THE SUBLIME PURITAN/*Milton and the Victorians*

The SUBLIME PURITAN

Milton and the Victorians

James G. Nelson

THE UNIVERSITY OF WISCONSIN PRESS · MADISON · 1963

Published by the University of Wisconsin Press
430 Sterling Court, Madison 6, Wisconsin

Copyright © 1963 by the Regents of the University of Wisconsin

Printed in the United States of America by
George Banta Company, Inc., Menasha, Wisconsin

Library of Congress Catalog Card Number 63–8438

To my Mother and Father

✒ Preface

LONG BEFORE the Age of Victoria, John Milton's "fit audience . . . though few" had burgeoned forth into legions of admirers who responded not only to his poetry but also to his striking personality and his forceful opinions on religion and politics. The history of this flowering, the rise of Milton's fame and influence in the eighteenth and early nineteenth centuries, has been told by John W. Good in his *Studies in the Milton Tradition* and by R. D. Havens in *The Influence of Milton on English Poetry*. But a detailed study of Milton's fortunes among the Victorians is not to be found. In fact, little else besides a few brief summaries of Milton's reputation during the period is in print. Certainly there is not enough detailed material to afford us the knowledge of Milton and the Victorians which we would wish to have. The present study, therefore, is an attempt to delineate the Victorian attitude toward Milton in order to bring the history of Milton's fame and influence up to the turn of the century, when Victorian criticism of the poet begins to merge with our own.

By the end of the nineteenth century, Milton had already become the special interest of the scholarly critic and poet, and such has he remained to the present day. And although the liveliness and quantity of modern Milton criticism attests to the fact that Milton's thought and art are still of great importance to us, the average reader has failed to exhibit much interest. This fact marks the major difference between modern and Victorian criticism. Whereas modern criticism tells us what Milton meant, Victorian criticism tells us what Milton meant to a whole society. And herein lies the peculiar interest which Victorian criticism has for us. Unlike our own, it is the response of a whole people, a kind of "portrait of an age," a picture of an uneasy, ever-changing society reacting to a great and significant figure. The Victorian attitude was, in a manner of speaking, a whole greater than its parts. That it was the voice of a whole age is more important than the fact that some opinions were biased and wrong-headed and that others were sound and suggestive.

The Victorian criticism of Milton is also interesting to us in that it affords us a basis for understanding the modern attitude. If the late nineteenth-century critics had not "divorced" Milton's thought from his art and if Walter Raleigh had not pictured _Paradise Lost_ as "a beautiful and grand curiosity," Pound and Eliot might not have been predisposed to ignore the thought and find the style and diction a hindrance to their own poetic efforts. Similarly if the Victorian notion of a stern Puritan Milton, a Milton who despite his Renaissance heritage became a symbol of the harsh Puritan temper, had not been given currency by Mark Pattison and others, the Christian Humanist critics of our time would have had little to react against. But aside from its obvious interest and importance, Victorian criticism of Milton stands as a monument to a man whose life and work represented positive values and artistic ideals which remained constant in an age of turbulent change.

Since we cannot know how the Victorians, in general, regarded Milton merely by studying what the critics said, or by laboriously tracing every instance of Miltonic influence that can be found in the poems of the period, this work is based on the assumption that the Victorian attitude toward Milton must be determined by a delineation and discussion of the dominant opinions, and the most significant views, be they notions promulgated by poets, critics, preachers, politicians, or laborers.

Since in my opinion the depth and the range of Milton materials in the Victorian period are so diverse and extensive that an all-inclusive work would demand what Walter Bagehot called the "exhaustive method," I have chosen to present a series of essays, each of which not only illuminates a significant facet of the Victorian attitude toward the "Prince of Poets," but also reflects to some extent the thought and disposition of the era from about 1820 to 1900. Naturally my great problem has been one of selection, but I hope that my familiarity with the materials has enabled me to choose and bring together the truly noteworthy opinions and responses which indicate to us the Victorian attitude toward Milton.

In the course of my work on this book, I have been most fortunate in having the encouragement and guidance of Professor Jerome Hamilton Buckley of Harvard University and Professor Marjorie Hope Nicolson of Columbia. Also I am grateful to Professor Dean Schmitter of Columbia University, and Professors Merritt Y. Hughes, Karl Kroeber, G. Thomas Tanselle, and Alvin Whitley of the University of Wisconsin, who read the manuscript and made valuable suggestions. For help on special problems, I want to thank Professor George Whalley of Queens University, Kingston, Ontario. For the reproductions of John Martin's illustrations of the 1827 edition of *Paradise Lost* I am indebted to the Newberry Library.

J. G. N.

Madison, Wisconsin
June, 1962

✍ Contents

✍ Illustrations

The illustrations are selected from the twenty-four mezzotints designed for the two-volume edition of *Paradise Lost* published by Septimus Prowett, London, 1827.

THE SUBLIME PURITAN/*Milton and the Victorians*

I ✍ A Power Amongst Powers

ANYONE WHO is familiar with the Victorians, the books they read, the literary, religious, and political figures they talked about, is tempted to believe that Thomas De Quincey was not exaggerating when in 1839 he said that John Milton "is not an author amongst authors, not a poet amongst poets, but a power amongst powers; and the 'Paradise Lost' is not a book amongst books, not a poem amongst poems, but a central force amongst forces."[1] Practically every person of consequence—poet, critic, preacher, statesman, or scientist—described his feelings and expressed his attitude toward Milton. To Tennyson he was the "mighty-mouth'd inventor of harmonies," the "God-gifted organ-voice of England";[2] to Matthew Arnold he was "the one artist of the highest rank in the great style whom we have."[3] Milton's words were to the matter-of-fact Macaulay "words of enchantment"; and when the promoter of "Fruit and Progress" read *Paradise Lost*, "new forms of beauty start[ed] at once into existence, and all the burial-places of the memory [gave] up their dead."[4] Speaking from his own experience, Thomas Keightley said, "The reading of *Paradise Lost* for the first time forms or should form, an era in the life of every one possessed of taste and poetic feeling." Almost as if he were speaking about the Bible, he said that since childhood, "the poetry of Milton has formed my constant study,—a source of delight in prosperity, of strength and consolation in adversity."[5] As late as 1894, Augustine Birrell, looking back over most of the period, was able to say of *Paradise Lost* that "no other poem can be mentioned which has so coloured English thought."[6]

This is high praise, indeed, but it is not unusual. To many, Milton was something like a saint whose relics were revered and whose poems were memorized and treasured up "to a life beyond life." For example, Elizabeth Barrett Browning felt "giddy" and was tempted to run her head "against the wall" when she viewed a first edition of *Paradise Lost* and saw Milton's signature and seal;[7] and her husband cherished a lock of Milton's hair which Leigh Hunt had given him. This, by the way, was that famous lock evidently taken from Milton's body when a coffin purported to be his was disinterred and rifled on August 4, 1790, in the church of St. Giles, Cripplegate.[8] When a physician gave the lock to Hunt, "he went into such rhapsodies that he composed no less than three sonnets addressed to the donor,"[9] and later when he showed the hair to John Keats, the young poet composed a poem on the spot.[10] Although Browning, who never had much to say about Milton, was not moved to compose as Hunt and Keats had been, he kept the lock in a glass-topped table cabinet near his desk, along with other precious keepsakes in his home at Warwick Crescent.

But other relics of Milton were evidently revered by persons of less fame, for in 1852, *Notes and Queries* published this interesting announcement: "In vol. V, p. 275, mention is made of Cromwell's skull; so it may not be out of place to tell you that I have handled one of Milton's ribs. Cowper speaks indignantly of the desecration of our divine poet's grave [in 'Stanzas on the late indecent Liberties taken with the remains of the great Milton. Anno 1790'] on which shameful occurrence some of the bones were clandestinely distributed. One fell to the lot of an old man and esteemed friend, and between forty-five and fifty years ago, at his house, not many miles from London, I have often examined the said rib-bone."[11]

Another interesting if less bizarre example of Milton's appeal was the response of the laboring class toward the poet. Today when few besides students of literature read *Paradise Lost,* we are somewhat surprised to learn that "poor and ignorant men could be found reading good books, *Pilgrim's Progress, Paradise Lost,* etc.,"[12] during the early Victorian period. Yet many among the lower classes who could read turned to *Paradise Lost* because of its religious content or because of Milton's republican tendencies. The most interesting example of a self-educated laborer who read Milton and revered his works is Thomas Cooper, the Chartist and writer, the son of a working dyer.

After his father's death, Cooper was apprenticed to a shoemaker. But like so many of his station, he passionately wanted an education. In his autobiography, he said that when he read *Paradise Lost* at the age of thirteen, he found it "above my culture and learning,"[13] but he was by no means discouraged, and thought that by the age of twenty-four he "might be able to master the elements of Latin, Greek, Hebrew, and French; might get well through Euclid, and through a course in algebra; might commit the entire 'Paradise Lost,' and seven of the best plays of Shakspeare, to memory." Perhaps these plans were a bit too ambitious, but Cooper made a valiant effort. His Sunday mornings were spent memorizing *Paradise Lost,* and as he repeated the lines daily, the "verse seemed to overawe" him. In time, "the perfection of his [Milton's] music, as well as the gigantic stature of the intellect," he wrote, "were fully perceived by my mind."[14]

Later Cooper became a leader of the extreme Chartist party, and in 1842 he was imprisoned in Stafford gaol for two years. While there he composed *The Purgatory of Suicides,* a political epic in ten books.[15] In Book II, he addressed Milton the patriot and lover of liberty who also was punished for his views: "Honour—all honour to thee, patriot bard!— / With whom I

took sweet counsel in my youth." Milton was the "Poet of Paradise,—whose glory illumed / My path of youthful penury." Re-
alizing that some of the long eulogy might not be clear, Cooper
in a note said, "In plain prose, I mean that my rehearsal of
Milton, during the long hours of darkness in my sleeping cell,
frequently converted the gloom into a season of ecstasy. I had
committed three books of 'Paradise Lost' to memory while at
the *last,* twenty years before my imprisonment; and I thus was
enabled to realize the high value of such an inalienable possession."[16]

Although there are numerous reports of persons who attempted to memorize *Paradise Lost,* just as Cooper did, one who
evidently succeeded was a Mr. Thomas Mason Jones, a lecturer
and writer, widely known in both England and America. A
newspaper story about his death in 1873 reported that it "is a
well-ascertained and carefully-verified record, that when quite a
young man, he [Jones] learned by heart the whole of 'Paradise
Lost,' and that he recited that prodigious epic in its entirety from
the commencing 'Of' to the final 'way' without book and without slip, omission, or blunder, at St. Martin's Hall, Long-acre,
and other places some years since. Whether his memory was
natural or acquired we know not, but the fact remains that he
knew 'Paradise Lost' by heart, and that he could repeat the
whole or any portion of it at call."[17]

Another lecturer somewhat better known to us than Mr. Jones
was Thomas Henry Huxley, "Darwin's Bulldog," who was anything but happy about the influence of *Paradise Lost.* But his
attitude toward Milton is yet another example of the varied impact of Milton upon the Victorians. Mark Pattison once said
that "the world he [Milton] created has taken possession of the
public mind," and he went on to note that "Huxley complains
that the false cosmogony, which will not yield to the conclusions of scientific research, is derived from the Seventh Book of
Paradise Lost, rather than from Genesis."[18] When Huxley lec-
tured in New York in 1876 at Chickering Hall, the New York
Tribune reported that on the first night, "punctual to the very

minute Professor Huxley came forward upon the platform, and was of course greeted with abundant applause. He laid a copy of Milton's *Paradise Lost* upon the reading desk; nothing else, neither manuscript nor notes." Then he proceeded to use *Paradise Lost* to illustrate the view that the world was specially created some 5,000 years ago. This led one New York newspaper, the *Sun,* to chide Huxley for burdening Milton, rather than Moses, with the theory of direct creation. ". . . instead of attacking Moses over the shoulders of John Milton," declared the reviewer, Huxley "should strike at Moses, face to face."[19]

Similarly, Dr. Edward Hitchcock, an American geologist whose attempts to determine the connection between geology and religion were well known in England and America, said in *The Religion of Geology* (1851) that Milton, in his *Paradise Lost,* had clothed the idea of an entire change throughout all organic nature "in a most graphic and philosophic dress; and probably his descriptions have done more than the Bible to give it currency. Indeed, could the truth be known, I fancy that on many points of secondary importance the current theology of the day has been shaped quite as much by the ingenious machinery of Paradise Lost as by the Scriptures; the theologians having so mixed up the ideas of Milton with those derived from inspiration, that they find it difficult to distinguish between them."[20]

Although Huxley had probably never warmed to *Paradise Lost* (at least in the right way), his master, Charles Darwin, once had. In his *Autobiography,* Darwin wrote: "Formerly Milton's *Paradise Lost* had been my chief favourite, and in my excursions during the voyage of the *Beagle,* when I could take only a single volume, I always chose Milton."[21]

Certainly the conflict between geology and Genesis alienated many from *Paradise Lost,* but not all. One of the most controversial but influential writers of the late Victorian period, the Positivist Frederic Harrison, in writing of the "Poets that I love," said:

> As I opened this paper with Dante, I end it with Milton—the English poet to whom I most often turn. . . . In the 'forties, at King's

College School, we had to learn by heart books of the *Paradise
Lost,* which we studied critically, with annotations, "parallel passages," and other stuff of the kind, which perhaps did us more
harm than good. At Wadham, on the appearance of my name in
the class list of Easter, 1853, the college presented me with the
Works of Milton, in the handsome edition of 1851, 8 vols. 8vo,
printed by William Pickering, from the original editions, with the
Life by John Mitford. . . . It has been my life-belt in the storms
of modern literature now for almost sixty years, though I fear it
has ruined my spelling for life, for the poet wrote—And justifie
the wayes of God to men. Years ago at Newton Hall I led a pilgrimage to visit the tomb of the poet in St. Giles', Cripplegate: and
on another occasion to the antique cottage at Chalfont to which he
retreated during the plague and wrote his *Paradise Regained.* To
Milton I say—

> What in me is dark illumine,
> What is low raise and support.[22]

The pilgrimage to Chalfont brings to mind another visit by a
poet who had little feeling for Milton, Dante Gabriel Rossetti.
On the first of September, 1842, he wrote to his mother from
Chalfont-St. Giles, "I saw Milton's house, which is unquestion-
ably the ugliest and dirtiest building in the whole village. It is
now occupied by a tailor." But the following July when he visited
the exhibition at Westminster Hall of cartoons for decorating
the new houses of Parliament, he was well impressed: "The
subjects are taken chiefly from English history. . . . A full third
of the exhibition (not to say more) is occupied by subjects
from Milton."[23] That Milton was and had been very popular
with the artists was, of course, not an unusual situation. Blake,
Fuseli, John Martin, J. M. W. Turner, Gustave Doré, had all
illustrated the great scenes in Milton's poems.

While the artists were poring over Milton's epic in search of
pictorial possibilities, the novelists and playwrights were in-
trigued by the many details of his life which had been or might
be enhanced and exploited in fiction. Although Milton's biography was fully known and filled with exciting episodes, truth
was not enough. There were many incidents which needed a
touch of romance and legend in order fully to satisfy the read-

ers' imagination. For instance, the Italian journey is the basis of two favorite Milton legends which were carried on by the Victorians: the interview with Galileo and the supposed love affair with Leonora Baroni.

In the *Areopagitica* Milton had said: "There it was that I found and visited the famous Galileo, grown old, a prisoner to the Inquisition for thinking otherwise than the Franciscan and Dominican licensers thought."[24] But what did the elegant young poet and the dying Galileo say to one another? Walter Savage Landor's famous account of the meeting in his *Imaginary Conversations* is well known, but there were more detailed and fanciful descriptions in Max Ring's novel, *John Milton and His Times*,[25] and in Major Vetch's play, *Milton at Rome*. In Ring's fiction, Milton meets Galileo at his villa near Florence and dines and converses at length with the sorrowful astronomer and his beautiful daughter, a nun. Galileo condemns the Inquisition and is heard to exclaim: "Nature was my Bible. I read it night and day without becoming tired of it. And could my efforts to recognize the Creator in His works be heresy?"[26] In a much more sensational and unhistorical account, Vetch transfers Galileo to a dungeon in the "bowels" of Rome, where after great danger and suspenseful encounters with suspicious and hostile forces of the Inquisition, a fearless and outspoken Milton visits him with reverence and awe.[27]

After visiting Galileo at Florence, the historical Milton went on to Rome, where he met the great Cardinal Barberini through the kindness of Lucas Holstenius, the Librarian of the Vatican. Milton in a letter to Holstenius acknowledged this and spoke of "that public musical entertainment" which he attended at Barberini's palace.[28] It was at this affair presented "with truly Roman magnificence" that Milton heard Leonora Baroni sing. But stories about a love affair between Milton and the singer were prominent throughout the eighteenth and nineteenth centuries. The legendary love affair, based primarily on the three Latin epigrams which Milton addressed to Leonora,[29] was soon linked with a legend which grew up at Cambridge about the handsome young Milton who while sleeping one day beneath a mulberry tree attracted the attention of a beautiful foreign lady who wrote a poem on the spot about his fair charms.

One of the most interesting uses of this legend is found in an atrocious poem of the young Bulwer-Lytton's college days called "Milton."[30] The poem opens with the Cambridge episode, but ends with an addition to the Leonora legend which is of Bulwer-Lytton's own devising: after Milton's death Leonora is observed kneeling at his tomb in great sorrow, bewailing the loss of her lover. Max Ring devotes a whole chapter of his novel to the meeting of Milton and Leonora at Cardinal Barberini's entertainment. None of the legendary accounts of this incident can compare with Ring's fully detailed and highly imaginative description of the event. The reading public's desire for flamboyant scenes dominated by voluptuous beauties is here exploited to the full. Needless to say, "indescribable feelings" filled the breast of young Milton when Leonora, resplendent in dark red, her raven hair wreathed with "flaming pomegranate-blossoms" ascended a gilded dais to sing "one of Palestrina's hymns."[31]

As one might suspect, Milton's domestic life, especially his relationship with Mary Powell, was not discreetly avoided by writers. Anne Manning's *The Maiden and Married Life of Mary Powell* and its sequel, *Deborah's Diary*,[32] leave little to be surmised. Mrs. Manning's book, with its intimate account of Milton's courtship at Forest Hill and his subsequent marriage, was very popular with the Victorians; having survived a powerful attack by De Quincey and having evoked an introduction which described it as "one of the most fragrant books in English literature," it took its place among the other classics in the Everyman's Library. While Mrs. Manning's fictional version of Mary Powell's life with Milton is not prejudicial to either Milton or Mary, Mrs. Jameson's discussion of the women in Milton's life in her *Memoirs of the Loves of the Poets* is openly hostile to Mary and the poet's elder daughters.[33] Milton, she contended, was throughout his entire life "peculiarly sensible to the charm of female society." As evidence, she pointed to his successive marriages, his friendship with Lady Margaret Ley, and "a thousand most lovely and glorious passages scattered through his works, which women may quote with triumph." In this entertaining account of Milton's love life, Dr. Johnson, "the Hippopotamus of literature," is banished to his den; Mary Powell, "that woman who embittered his [Milton's] life for fourteen or fifteen years," is scorned; and Milton's elder daughters are compared to Goneril and Regan.

In numerous other novels and plays, references to Milton reflect various aspects of the popular attitude toward him. In George Eliot's *Middlemarch,* in which his name is frequently mentioned, he is identified with Casaubon. For example, before her marriage Dorothea "felt sure that she would have accepted the judicious Hooker, if she had been born in time to save him from that wretched mistake he made in matrimony; or John Milton when his blindness had come on; or any of the other great men whose odd habits would have been glorious piety to endure." After her marriage, however, Dorothea thought "that she could have been patient with John Milton, but she had never imagined him behaving in this way."[34] And, indeed, later, Peter Bayne felt that "a Dorothea Brooke and a John Milton might . . . have realized an ideally perfect marriage union."[35]

Although the comments which I have cited here tend to indicate an almost wholly favorable opinion of the poet, there can be no doubt that through the years the Victorian response to Milton ran the gamut of emotions from the enthusiastic admiration of Thomas Macaulay and Walter Savage Landor to the aversion of Hurrell Froude and William Morris. As we shall see, the dissenters, Evangelicals, and Whigs were generally lavish in their praise of the poet, and often made it a point "to commemorate, in all love and reverence, the genius and virtues of John Milton, the poet, the statesman, the philosopher, the glory of English literature, the champion and martyr of English liberty."[36] But the High Churchmen, Catholics, and Tories frequently damned him with faint praise or with outright scorn and disapproval. The Rev. Robert Willmott's life of Milton is typical of High Church commentary in that it praises Milton as "our sublimest poet" while it sorrows "over the darker pages of his life," especially the Commonwealth years.[37] Both John Henry Newman and John Keble allowed their disapprobation of Milton to influence their opinion of his poetry; and Hurrell Froude, their close associate in the Oxford Movement, wrote, "I am glad I know something of the Puritans, as it gives me a better right to hate Milton."[38] Years later, Gerard Manley Hopkins, who prized Milton's art, was of the opinion that Milton was "a bad man."[39]

This variety of opinion, this spirited response—these are the signs which mark Milton as a real force in the Victorian Period. Only a man whose ideas were still vital and alive and whose personal image still loomed large in the minds of the nation could have provoked such a multiplicity of opinion uttered in many instances with such passion. Because Milton's art and ideals were still current, they were of considerable use to those who found them congenial and of great concern to those who found them subversive.

De Quincey's declaration that Milton was "a power amongst powers" is, therefore, sound. Certainly for Victorians of widespread influence Milton was considerably more than a "poet amongst poets." To Macaulay, the eminent historian of Protestant and Whig interests, Milton was the great symbolic figure of the Reformation and the Glorious Revolution; to Matthew Arnold, the ardent champion of the cultural and literary traditions of the Western world, Milton was the English prototype of the classic spirit. Milton, like all powerful figures, was loved by many, hated by some, but ignored by few.

II ☞ Shakespeare and Milton

Shakspeare is the Spinozistic deity—an
omnipresent creativeness. Milton is the deity of
prescience; he stands ab extra. . . .

—COLERIDGE, *Table Talk*

IN THE nineteenth century, Milton and Shakespeare occupied "the two glory-smitten summits of the poetic mountain,"[1] and although we today agree, we seldom think of comparing and contrasting these poets so often as our nineteenth-century forebears did. Our attitude, however, is not that of the Romantics and Victorians whose mania for pairing off artists—Tennyson versus Browning, Dickens versus Thackeray—often led them to contrast Shakespeare and Milton when they thought (as they often did) of two opposing schools of poetry. Throughout most of the nineteenth century Milton was the model of the poet whose life was mirrored in his work; Shakespeare was the supreme exemplar of the poet who lost himself in the vivid characters of his dramas.

The tendency of Romantic and Victorian critics to separate literature into two distinct kinds and to utilize Shakespeare and Milton as the exemplars[2] is in many ways analogous to the German preoccupation in the 1790's with the problem of ancient and modern literature. Since the early days of sentimental and emotional *Sturm und Drang,* the German literati had been painfully aware that they were living in a world wholly different from that of Homer and the Greeks of antiquity. Moreover, they believed that a shift in sensibility was clearly apparent in their literature. The serene, cheerful equilibrium and oneness with nature, which they attributed to the ancients, had produced an objective art of classic beauty, but this disposition had given way to modern man's troubled awareness of self, his alienation from nature, and a necessarily subjective art. Friedrich Schlegel, torn between the aesthetic ideals of the two literatures, in an attempt to comprehend this strange mutation in the world of art, divided poetry into "die interessante Poesie" (later to be called "romantische") which was characteristically subjective, and "die Schöne Poesie" which was characterized by its objective beauty. Another great critic, Friedrich Schiller, also based his famous critical document, "On Naive and Sentimental Poetry," on this apparent shift in sensibility which separated the ancients from the moderns, and like Schlegel partitioned the realm of literature into two distinct areas.

In this essay, Schiller, echoing Herder's ideas about primitive races and Wincklemann's "Apollonian" view of Greek culture, declared that there were two kinds of poetry—sentimental and naive—"which embrace and exhaust the entire field. All poets . . . will belong, according to the time when they flourish, according to the accidental circumstances that have influenced their education generally, and the different dispositions of mind through which they pass," to the order of one or the other.[3] Naive poetry is objective, realistic, and limited in scope; sentimental poetry is subjective and idealistic, and its scope is of infinite magnitude.

In this analysis of the literary situation of his day, Schiller saw history as a steady progress from a state of nature to a state of civilization and artificiality. Man, he said, in a state of innocence was wholly attuned to nature, obeyed his instincts, and acted spontaneously in accordance with the inner laws of his own being. But as civilization advanced, as cultures became more artificial, man became alienated from nature and was unable to respond spontaneously and intuitively to her prompt-ings. For reason and free will, he exchanged happiness and perfection, and, thereby, exposed himself "to so many combats with [himself], to so many anxieties and errors."[4] However, the naive poets—the ancient Greeks and a very few fortunate and happy spirits of the modern world such as Shakespeare and Goethe—are still a part, so to speak, of nature and are yet able to live in harmony with all things. As a result, the poetry of Homer and Shakespeare is endowed with a calm simplicity and spontaneity of expression utterly alien to the poetry of modern or sentimental poets.

While Schiller considers Shakespeare a naive poet, he de-scribes Milton as a sentimental poet who like himself is aware that "the harmony of feeling and thought" which man once possessed is now outside himself and exists only "in an *ideal* state." Milton's "magnificent picture of the first human pair, and of the state of innocence in paradise, [is] the most beautiful idyl . . . of the sentimental kind."[5]

During the eighteenth century, critics more often than not focused their attention on the similarities between Shakespeare and Milton rather than on their divergent qualities. For example, Edward Young, still fighting the battle of the Ancients and the Moderns in his *Conjectures on Original Composition* (1759), praises Shakespeare and Milton as great "modern" poets who possessed "original" as opposed to "imitative" genius.[6] But Schiller, whose account of Shakespeare is colored by the eighteenth-century concept of the "natural," "original" poet,[7] is clearly concerned with the differences between Shakespeare and Milton, and in his discussion of naive and sentimental poetry approximates the characteristic nineteenth-century view. In particular, Schiller's notion that the naive poet is "objective" in that he "hides himself behind his work" and, in this respect, is "like the Diety behind this universe,"[8] suggests Coleridge's emphasis on Shakespeare, the selfless, impersonal poet who was able to dart himself forth and pass "into all the forms of hu-man character and passion." To Coleridge, Shakespeare was "the one Proteus of the fire and flood." Milton, on the other hand, "attracts all forms and things to himself, into the unity of his own ideal. All things and modes of action," said Coleridge, "shape themselves anew in the being of Milton, while Shakspeare becomes all things, yet forever remaining himself."[9]

Although Coleridge always refrained from specifically subordinating Milton to Shakespeare, the superiority of the one over the other is clearly implied in at least one respect—that of imaginative power.[10] Shakespeare, Coleridge thought, had the highest order of imagination which enabled him to bring all his abilities and mental resources into a perfectly harmonious state in which no one aspect of the poet's self was dominant, not even his personality. Shakespeare's impersonality was a product of an incredibly powerful imaginative process which produced a fully active self, a kind of super-self bound up in pure action and pure being.

Extraordinary though they were, Milton's powers of imagination, on the other hand, were less. Though at times he could rise beyond self, like Shakespeare, to the heights of impersonal creativity, his genius could not often strike the imaginative balance in which personality and will are blended into a harmonious whole. Consequently, Milton's powerful mind and forceful personality intrude and interfere with our comprehension of his work. Thus, the fundamental distinction between the two poets in Coleridge's estimation is that the one is what might be called an impersonal artist, whereas the other is a "self-centered" one.

This characteristic nineteenth-century view found in Coleridge is also present in Hazlitt's critical works, especially in those essays in which he describes Shakespeare's sympathetic imagination. Shakespeare, said Hazlitt, "was the least of an egotist that it was possible to be";[11] he had the ability preeminent to identify himself with others and become absorbed in the object of his contemplation. Through the sympathetic character of his imagination, Shakespeare could feel intensely what Falstaff felt, or see with the eyes of an Iago, or suffer the torments of a Lear. Hazlitt's criticism of Shakespeare returns again and again to this point, and it is just at this point where he, in Hazlitt's view, differs most from Milton. For Milton possessed what Hazlitt called "genius in ordinary," which is "a more obstinate and less versatile thing."[12] Consequently, the bias and opinion of the poet are, in Hazlitt's view, apparent in all his work. While Shakespeare "is only the vehicle for the sentiments of his characters," Hazlitt concluded, Milton's characters "are only a vehicle for his own."[13]

Since Shakespeare was able to transcend self through the power of his imagination, he became, so to speak, that which *is.* His creative moments were states of pure being in which the universal was attained. That is what Hazlitt meant when he said: "The striking peculiarity of Shakespeare's mind was its generic quality, its power of communication with all other minds—so that it contained a universe of thought and feeling within itself, and had no one peculiar bias, or exclusive excellence more than another. He was just like any other man, but that he was like all other men."[14] But Milton "thought of nobler forms and nobler things than those he found about him. He lived apart, in the solitude of his own thoughts, carefully excluding from his mind whatever might distract its purposes or alloy its purity, or damp its zeal."[15]

This contrast between Milton and Shakespeare which often, I suspect, helped critics inform themselves and their readers about Shakespeare's rather enigmatic personality by juxtaposing it with the more familiar mind of Milton, came to be widely accepted during the nineteenth century. It is not unusual to come across passages at random in which authors draw the comparison for its own sake or to illuminate some other point. For instance, in his *Life of Schiller,* Carlyle could not describe the famous first meeting between Goethe and Schiller without comparing it to a hypothetical meeting between Shakespeare and Milton. As a result, the whole passage is actually a contrast between the sentimental poets, Schiller and Milton, and the naive poets, Goethe and Shakespeare. "How gifted, how diverse in their gifts!" he exclaimed. "The mind of one plays calmly, in its capricious and inimitable graces, over all the provinces of human interest; the other concentrates powers as vast, but far less various, on a few subjects; the one is catholic, the other is sectarian." The first, he declared, "is endowed with an all-comprehending spirit" which allows "men and things of every shape and hue to have their own free scope in his conception, as they have it in the world where Providence has placed them." The other, on the contrary, "is earnest, devoted; struggling with a thousand mighty projects of improvement; feeling more intensely as he feels more narrowly." Such a being is "dissatisfied, impetuous," and is scarcely able to conceive the possibility of a state of eternal rest. "Apart from the difference of their opinions and mental structure," Carlyle concluded, "Shakespeare and Milton seem to have stood in some such relation as this to each other, in regard to the primary structure of their minds."[16]

Although Coleridge, Hazlitt, and Carlyle compared Shakespeare with Milton in order to better understand the true nature of his genius, and seldom if ever to judge the one superior to the other, it is apparent that these critics honored Shakespeare's impersonal art more than what they considered to be the subjective art of Milton. Theoretically, Shakespeare's "all-comprehending spirit" appealed to them in a way which Milton's more rigorous, less catholic, attitude of mind did not. Yet, in actuality, there can be no doubt that the "earnest, devoted" Milton, "struggling with a thousand mighty projects of improvement; feeling more intensely as he feels more narrowly" was far more closely akin to Carlyle and his contemporaries than Shakespeare ever could have been.

Because the Victorians could see a great part of Milton's political and personal history embodied in the characters and incidents of his work, because he was more immediately knowable, Milton was a living figure to be argued, praised, and blamed in virtually every area of their intellectual and artistic thought. The same was not true of Shakespeare in Victorian times. Without doubt, he had qualities which they never tired of admiring, qualities which they wished they had the leisure and the stable world to enjoy, but it was the mental attitude of Milton, his sense of commitment to problems which in many ways were akin to those which pressed the Victorians, that instantly marked him out as a kindred spirit, one with whom they could converse.

For this reason, the constant comparison of Shakespeare with Milton during the period is misleading, and, in fact, reveals a tendency on the part of the Victorians to praise objective art and at the same time demand of themselves and others a personal involvement in the problems of the day. One need but to recall Arnold's 1853 Preface to be convinced of the contemporary demand for a literature concerned with timely subjects.[17] Yearn though they would for a world in which they could occupy a more aloof, less involved, position, Carlyle, Tennyson, even Arnold himself, emulated Milton, who turned his back on Greece and came home to be of service to his country.

III ✒ The Miltonic Sonnet

> . . . and when a damp
> Fell round the path of Milton, in his hand
> The Thing became a trumpet; whence he blew
> Soul-animating strains—alas, too few!
>
> —WORDSWORTH, "Scorn not the Sonnet"

I

ESPITE THE fact that the Victorians theoretically preferred the objective art of Shakespeare to the subjective art of Milton, and in so doing openly repudiated their natural tendency toward subjectivism, they were, like Schiller, frustrated because they could not seek Shakespeare in his plays, "meet his heart," and "reflect with him in his theme."[1] As David Masson expressed it: "We seek . . . to penetrate into his heart—to detect and to fix in everlasting portraiture that mood of his soul which was ultimate and characteristic; in which, so to speak, he came ready-fashioned from the Creator's hands."[2]

Since Shakespeare in his dramas could shift with apparent ease through an immense succession of masks, the critic's attempt to detect the poet's personal bent and peculiarities was dangerous and largely unrewarding. But, in this case, Masson declared,

all the world ought to know, there *is* a positive and ascertained clue. Shakespeare has left to us not merely a collection of dramas, the exercises of his creative phantasy in a world of ideal matter, but also certain poems which are assuredly and expressly autobiographic. Criticism seems now pretty conclusively to have determined, what it ought to have determined long ago, that the *Son-*

nets of Shakespeare are, and can possibly be, nothing else than a poetical record of his own feelings and experience—a connected series of entries, as it were, in his own diary—during a certain period of his London life.[3]

Actually, the possibility of reading Shakespeare's poems autobiographically had attracted little attention before the first quarter of the nineteenth century. Then Wordsworth in England and the Schlegels in Germany found it quite plausible that Shakespeare did "give an account of himself" in his sonnets.[4] Once the Romantics had opened the way to a biographical reading of the poems, the Victorians, for the most part, followed their lead. Although Robert Browning protested and a few critics scorned the allurement, the critics from Thomas Carlyle to Walter Raleigh and A. C. Bradley agreed with Masson that the sonnets of Shakespeare "*are* autobiographic—distinctly, intensely, painfully autobiographic, although in a style and after a fashion of autobiography so peculiar, that we can cite only Dante in his *Vita Nuova,* and Tennyson in his *In Memoriam,* as having furnished precisely similar examples of it."[5]

That the Victorians were afflicted with a double personality —a public aspect which avowed loyalty to an objective art, and a private one which craved subjective literature—is well illustrated by their praise of Shakespeare's universality—his "many-sidedness" and his ability to lose himself in his art—and their preoccupation with the biographical relationship between Shakespeare and his sonnets. Indeed, the search for biography was so intense during the nineteenth century that the work of the poet was often overshadowed by the poet himself. However, this biographical reading of Shakespeare's sonnets was in keeping with a Victorian tendency to regard the sonnet as ideal for conveying the poet's personal feelings. If poetry in general should be approached objectively, the Victorians were not averse to excepting the sonnet form and reserving it for a brief indulgence of a subjective mood. The sonnet is justified, according to Mark Pattison, by the "fugitive nature of the poetic mood,—the impossibility for both poet and hearer of sustaining intense emotion, or fixing evanescent impressions for any length of time."[6]

Thus, in the nineteenth century, Shakespeare joined Milton in the ranks of the subjective poets when he was considered as a writer of sonnets; and although Shakespeare's sonnets received more critical attention because of the mad search for the identity of Mr. W. H., the dark lady, and the rival poet, Milton's sonnets were more often imitated and generally preferred to those of Shakespeare.

II During the eighteenth-century, the major critics came close to reading the sonnet out of the English language. George Steevens, the editor of Shakespeare, defined it as a "metrical whim . . . composed in the highest strain of affectation, pedantry, circumlocution and nonsense"; and after declaring its constituent parts to be "quaintness, obscurity, and tautology," he wished the sonnet had "expired in the country where it was born."[7] Moreover, his close friend, Dr. Johnson, who disliked the form intensely, believed that it was "not very suitable to the English language."[8] The eighteenth-century aversion was so strong that the sonnets of Shakespeare and Milton were slighted and disparaged.[9]

Nineteenth-century critics, however, completely reversed the eighteenth-century opinion of the sonnet, and gave it serious, sympathetic, and, at times, enthusiastic consideration. Poets from Wordsworth and Keats to Dante Rossetti and Gerard Manley Hopkins employed the sonnet form often and well, and helped establish a vogue which approximated, at least in quantity, the sonnet "craze" of the late sixteenth century. Furthermore, the sonnets of Shakespeare and Milton were at last given the critical attention that they deserved. The nineteenth century hailed Shakespeare's sonnets because they were the only personal or subjective poems which he wrote, and prized Milton's as more intensely, more immediately, personal than any of his other poems. But what is of special importance is the fact that the Victorians believed that Milton's sonnets were the finest in English.

When the fortunes of the sonnet began to revive, especially after Wordsworth's extensive use of the form, the sonnets of Milton rather than those of the Elizabethans became the model. The poets' practice was confirmed and supported by the critics who stated their objections to the Elizabethan sonnet quite clearly. The whole group of sonneteers from Sidney and Spenser to Samuel Daniel and Shakespeare were charged with writing sonnets which were frivolous, obscure, artificial, ingenious, and lacking in genuine emotion. It is quite obvious that what the nineteenth-century critics really objected to was the Petrarchan *matter*—the courtly love motif, the extensive use of conceit, paradox, and complex imagery—which gave the Elizabethan sonnet its special character; but, at the same time, they condemned the Elizabethans also because they disregarded the Petrarchan *form*. Milton's sonnets, on the other hand, were serious, simple and direct, lucid, emotionally genuine, and closer to the Petrarchan form than any other sonnets in English.[10]

Milton, of course, had begun his career as a sonnet writer in the "Petrarchian" tradition. The early poem "O Nightingale" and the Italian sonnets amply illustrate his mastery of the conventional themes and elements of this highly artificial verse form. But later, when he became deeply involved in the political and religious controversies of the Civil War, he turned away from the courtly love motif which had dominated the Italian and Elizabethan sonnet to the sonnet of denunciation of public wrongs and the sonnet of compliment to friends—both of which had been employed by Petrarch and other Italian sonneteers. Furthermore, Milton, at this time, turned away from Petrarch's arrangement of sentences and passed on to the freer, more varied sentence structure of Giovanni della Casa.[11] Although he continued to employ the Petrarchan rhyme scheme, he disregarded Petrarch's fixed pauses and closed quatrains and made striking use of enjambement.

While the sonnets which Milton wrote over a period of

nearly thirty years sometimes celebrate the personal valor of Fairfax and Cromwell, they never commemorate the coyness of a mistress or the wiles of Cupid. Nothing could be further from the tone and subject matter of the Petrarchan tradition than Milton's finest sonnet, "On the Late Massacre in Piedmont." The stern vehemence of expression, the earnest tone, the plain yet dignified vocabulary, and the sonnet form itself combine to channel Milton's bitter, indignant emotions into a trumpet-call totally alien to the flute-like quality of the Elizabethan sonnet.

When the Victorians found themselves in a position somewhat like that of Milton—in the midst of reform bills at home and revolutions abroad, dissatisfaction within the Church and threats of disestablishment without—they, too, preferred sonnet themes better suited to the serious and morally earnest frame of mind which the turbulent and uneasy years of the early Victorian period demanded.[12] In addition, they insisted upon a straightforward, lucid sonnet style, and a genuinely personal subject matter. For example, Hazlitt preferred Milton's sonnets because they had more of "this personal and internal character than any other. . . . I do not know," he wrote, "indeed but they may be said to be almost the first effusions of this sort of natural and personal sentiment in the language." Sidney's sonnets were censured by Hazlitt for being "elaborately quaint and intricate and more like riddles than sonnets." Similarly, Shakespeare's sonnets were condemned because they had no "leading, prominent idea," and because they were "overcharged and monotonous." "As to their ultimate drift," concluded Hazlitt, "I can make neither head nor tail of it."[13]

Charles Lamb's criticism of Sidney is much the same. Sidney's sonnets, said Lamb, "fall below the plain moral dignity, the sanctity, and high yet modest spirit of self-appraisal, of Milton, in his compositions of a similar structure. They are in truth what Milton, censuring the Arcadia, says of the work, . . . 'vain and amatorious.' " Sidney's sonnets are, according to Lamb, "stuck full of amorous fancies—far-fetched conceits."[14] Like-

wise, Henry Hallam, the historian, in his critique of Shakespeare's sonnets, went so far as to say that "it is impossible not
to wish that Shakespeare had never written them. There is," he
continued, "a weakness and folly in all excessive and misplaced
affection which is not redeemed by the touches of nobler sentiments that abound in this long series of sonnets. . . . The obscurity is often such as only conjecture can penetrate; . . . and
so many frigid conceits are scattered around, that we might almost fancy the poet to have written without genuine emotion,
did not such a host of other passages attest the contrary." But
Hallam commended "the majestic simplicity, the holy calm"
that ennoble the sonnets of Milton.[15] As late as 1880 James
Ashcroft Noble, in an article entitled "The Sonnet in England,"
noted with some distress that the "pre-Miltonic sonnet had certainly been largely devoted to the elaboration of amorous fan-
tasies,"[16] and he hastened to quote approvingly Landor's lines
to the effect that Milton

> Caught the
> Sonnet from the dainty hand
> Of Love, who cries to lose it, and he gave
> The notes to glory.
>
> ("To the President of the French Republic")

In short, Milton's sonnets were popular and highly esteemed
because the readers preferred a sonnet which created a tone of
earnest sincerity as a fitting background for an intimate, personal subject matter presented in a simple, clear, dignified manner. But of these two important elements—the personal utterance and the plain, direct style—the one more highly prized
was the personal note. In the eighteenth century, Johnson had
readily "dispatched" Milton's "little pieces . . . without much
anxiety," but the Victorians, who often condemned Milton for
being too subjective in his other works, praised his sonnets precisely because they were so very intimate. For, said Macaulay,
although Milton's "peculiar character . . . may be found in all
his works," it is "most strongly displayed in the sonnets. . . .
Those remarkable poems," he continued,

have been undervalued by critics who have not understood their nature. . . . There is none of the ingenuity of Filicaja in the thought, none of the hard and brilliant enamel of Petrarch in style. They are simple but majestic records of the feelings of the poet; as little tricked out for the public eye as his diary would have been. A victory, an unexpected attack upon the city, a momentary fit of depression or exultation, a jest thrown out against one of his books, a dream which for a short time restored to him that beautiful face over which the grave had closed for ever, led him to musings, which without effort shaped themselves into verse. The unity of sentiment and severity of style which characterise these little pieces remind us of the Greek Anthology, or perhaps still more of the Collects of the English Liturgy. The noble poem on the Massacres of Piedmont is strictly a collect in verse.[17]

James Montgomery, too, was speaking for his generation when he said that "Milton is never more himself than when he speaks of himself. Here [in the sonnet on his blindness] we are let into the inmost sanctuary of his mind."[18] James Noble wrote that even "when Milton's matter repels or fails to interest, there is always something in his manner which compels an attentive and fascinated hearing. The personal quality, which was of pure and high self-containedness all compact, informs the language and gives it a magical power."[19]

Not only were Milton's sonnets subjective, they were simple and dignified. Aubrey de Vere, the younger, a critic as well as a practitioner of the sonnet, thought that Shakespeare's sonnets were better described as "exquisite short poems" because they did not have "the still and lustrous simplicity" which is characteristic of Milton's and Wordsworth's sonnet's.[20] De Vere went on to say that his father "valued the sonnet more because its austere brevity, its severity, and its majestic completeness fit it especially for the loftier themes of song. . . . A true sonnet is characterized by greatness, not prettiness." Furthermore, the sonnet, despite the addition of rhyme, "demands, like the Miltonic blank verse, a nobler music varying from the amplest to the subtlest cadences of diction strong, pure, felicitous, and lucid."[21]

An interesting example of a typical Victorian view is provided for us in an imaginary conversation from the pages of an 1880 number of *Blackwood's Edinburgh Magazine*.[22] One evening three "typical Victorians"—Geoffrey, Basil, and Henry—decide to pass the time by trying to pick the "six grandest sonnets in the English language." After considerable debate, Geoffrey declares that there are "two classes of the English sonnet; the more loosely organised,—at the head of which must stand Shakespeare's,—and the more closely coherent, the type for which are Milton's; but," Geoffrey continues, "I cannot possibly consider the first class, whatever its merits may be, as fulfilling the requirements of the Sonnet in the way in which Petrarch conceived them, and Milton and Wordsworth (in their happier efforts) accomplished them." Basil, somewhat surprised, inquires, "Then you will give your vote, when we come to select our six, against even one of Shakespeare's best?" and Geoffrey replies: "Decidedly. They none of them impress my mind as do Milton's; they lack his stately grandeur, and fail to give the same satisfactory sense of perfect finish. They may be perfect in their own line, but it is a line in point of art, laid on a lower level than Milton's."[23]

The classic statement of the Victorian attitude toward the sonnet, however, was made by Mark Pattison, who in his lengthy introduction to *The Sonnets of John Milton* (1883) summarized and brought to fruition the views and inclinations of previous nineteenth-century commentators. Writing as if he were a literary dictator, Pattison began his discussion of the sonnet by laying down a multitude of strict, formal rules for the sonnet and spelling out in great detail what was and was not permissible in its composition.[24] For example, Pattison outlawed the couplet ending when he stated that the "two last lines of a sonnet must not rime together. The principle of the sonnet structure is continuity of thought and metre; the final couplet interrupts the flow, it stands out by itself as an independent member of the construction; the wave of emotion, instead of being carried on to an even subsidence, is abruptly checked and broken as against a barrier." The conclusion of the sonnet, he continued, should always avoid "anything like epi-grammatic point."[25]

Another aspect of the sonnet that Pattison severely con-demned was obscurity, which, he wrote, "is a fault in any writ-ing, prose or verse. But in a short poem, such as a sonnet, an obscure line is not only lost itself, it diffuses dimness over the whole piece. . . . Notwithstanding the obviousness of this fault, it became the commonest error of the early sonneteers. Shake-speare's sonnets are largely infected by an obscurity arising from over-ingenuity."[26] Since the sonnet demands simplicity, "the feeling intended to be impressed must be immediately conveyed, and not buried away beyond comprehension in a con-torted thought uttered in enigmatical language."[27]

It was Pattison's opinion that Shakespeare should not have employed the sonnet at all, because "it was a form in which his superabounding force strangled itself." Furthermore, Shake-speare's example had been a "misleading influence on our son-nettists. . . . If it had been recognized that the so-called sonnets of Shakspeare are not sonnets at all, . . . but a continuous poem, or poems, written in fourteen-line stanzas, as Tennyson's *In Memoriam* is, largely, in sixteen-line stanzas, how much mis-placed skill would have been saved!"[28] In other words, the son-net should not depend on what goes before or after it. A sonnet which depends upon a sequence for its meaning loses its in-dividuality and becomes a stanza in a poem.

When Pattison finally came to a discussion of Milton, he declared that the poet was forever distinguished in the annals of the sonnet, because "he emancipated this form of poem from the two vices which depraved the Elizabethan Sonnet— from the vice of misplaced wit in substance, and of misplaced rime in form. He recognized that the sonnet belonged to the poetry of feeling, and not to the poetry of ingenuity. And he saw that the perfection of metrical construction was not reached by tacking together three four-line verses rounded by a couplet at the end."[29]

Although Pattison condemned Milton's sonnets because the

relation of the lines to the sentences was not strictly Petrarchan, his praise far outweighed the blame.[30] And when it came to comparing the Miltonic sonnet with the Elizabethan, Pattison again clearly demonstrated the Victorian preference:

> The effectiveness of Milton's sonnets is chiefly due to the *real* nature of the character, person, or incident of which each is the delineation. Each person, thing, or fact, is a moment in Milton's life, on which he was stirred; sometimes in the soul's depths, sometimes on the surface of feeling, but always truly moved. He found the sonnet enslaved to a single theme, that of unsuccessful love, mostly a simulated passion. . . . And what is here felt powerfully, is expressed directly and simply. The affectation of the Elizabethan sonnet, its elaborate artifice, is discarded, and replaced by a manly straightforwardness. It is a man who is speaking to us, not an artist attitudinizing to please us. . . . We never for a moment feel the suspicion that Milton may be feigning or forcing a sentiment, as we now and then suspect Petrarch or Shakspeare.[31]

III   "All English writers of sonnets have imitated Milton," said Francis Jeffrey in 1807;[32] and although Jeffrey was being a bit dogmatic, as he often was, the sonnet since Milton had definitely taken its direction from him. When Wordsworth chose to imitate the Miltonic sonnet and lend it his prestige, a major sonnet tradition was firmly established which extended far into the Victorian era and was in many ways antithetical to the sonnets of the period best known today, those of Elizabeth Barrett Browning and Dante Rossetti, which derived their inspiration from the Elizabethan and Italian sonneteers rather than from Milton.

As one might expect, the Miltonic sonnet of the Victorian period had its impetus in emotionally disturbing events such as the Oxford Movement or the tense political repercussions on the Continent in 1848, and, therefore, was most often devoted to religious or political themes. For instance, John Henry Newman, John Keble, and other Tractarians turned to the sonnet in their moments of crisis. According to George Sanderlin, Keble's sonnets "are Miltonic in their deep feeling and high principle; their denunciatory quality recalls the Milton of 'On the Late

Massacre in Piedmont.' . . . Newman's resemble Milton's more
in restraint and fidelity to the feeling inspiring them."[33]

Similarly, the Miltonic sonnet served as the accepted model
for the political sonnet of the 1830's and 1840's.[34] The years
which brought the reform bills and the waves of liberalism and
reaction also brought a series of political sonnets written by
young men in moments of liberal zeal. Tennyson, Arnold, Rossetti, and Swinburne naturally turned to Milton's sonnets for a
guide when they wished to denounce the forces of reaction and
repression. Milton, the republican, the ardent advocate of freedom, who had condemned the tyrant and upheld liberty and
truth in his sonnets was, they believed, a kindred spirit.

Actually, the prototype of the political sonnet was often
Milton's "On the Late Massacre in Piedmont," which had a
tremendous vogue among the Victorians. It is the sonnet most
directly imitated and most often praised and analyzed; and,
therefore, it is not surprising that our imaginary conversational-
ists were led in their search for the six best sonnets to the "Piedmont" sonnet. For instance, when Basil asked Henry and Geoffrey which two of Milton's sonnets they preferred above all
others, Henry replied, "The one on his blindness, and that on
the 'Massacre of the Waldenses.' But then, I know them by
heart; some of the others I only know slightly, if at all." Geoffrey agreed and hastened to eulogize: "What concentrated
power there is in that on the Piedmontese Martyrs! With what
few vigorous strokes it paints to us the ancient faith, the simple
life, the mountain habitation, the undeserved sufferings of those
hapless confessors whose

>   'moans
> The vales redoubled to the hills, and they
> To Heaven.' "

Basil, a bit pedantically, chimed in: "Do you notice the added
force given by alliteration to the lines immediately preceding
which tell us how the bloody persecutors

>   'rolled
> Mother with infant down the *rocks?*'

and the way in which that verse seems to make us hear the fall of the victims; and to hold our breath with horror as we watch them reach their sad resting place, and lie motionless, shattered and dead, at the foot of the precipice!"[35]

If this conversation is too contrived, the element of high and sincere praise is common. Landor called the sonnet a "magnificent psalm, . . . the noblest of Sonnets."[36] And Mark Pattison said that in this particular sonnet "is realised Wordsworth's definition of poetry: 'The spontaneous overflow of powerful feeling.' "[37] Perhaps James Noble best summarized the opinion of the Victorians when he declared:

> The great sonnet "on the late Massacres in Piedmont," is one of those achievements in which matter of the noblest order moulds itself a form of the highest excellence, matter and form being, as in music and all supreme art, so bound up and interfused, that though we know both of them to be there, we cannot know them or think of them apart. Much has been said in eulogy of this sonnet, and said worthily and well; but there is a perfection which mocks praise, and it is this perfection that is here attained; not the perfection which consists in this quality or that, but which comes when all qualities which may be displayed, all potentialities which can be exerted, meet in triumphant, satisfying, utter accomplishment. When Lord Macaulay called it a "collect in verse" he was on the right track, . . . but it would have been safer to compare it to some great work of nature.

In addition, Noble noticed its "splendid and sonorous rhetoric, the solemn majesty as of a judge pronouncing doom, the white heat of prophetic passion." This sonnet then concludes, he wrote, "with a line so weighty and sonorous that it reminds us of an avalanche thundering down the side of one of his 'Alpine mountains cold.' "[38]

The young Tennyson who rang the church bells in celebration of the passage of the first Reform Bill and went to Spain with Arthur Hallam to help the rebels was not so conventional and conservative as he later appeared to some of his critics. Early he caught the tone of Milton's trumpet in the sonnet on the Polish insurrection of 1830.[39] But of all the sonnets written in imitation of "Piedmont," perhaps the best is Tennyson's

"Montenegro" published in 1877, the most Miltonic of his sonnets and the one he himself preferred to all his others.

> They rose to where their sovran eagle sails,
> They kept their faith, their freedom, on the height,
> Chaste, frugal, savage, arm'd by day and night
> Against the Turk; whose inroad nowhere scales
> Their headlong passes, but his footstep fails,
> And red with blood the Crescent reels from fight
> Before their dauntless hundreds, in prone flight
> By thousands down the crags and thro' the vales.
> O smallest among peoples! rough rock-throne
> Of Freedom! warriors beating back the swarm
> Of Turkish Islam for five hundred years,
> Great Tsernogora! never since thine own
> Black ridges drew the cloud and brake the storm
> Has breathed a race of mightier mountaineers.

The Miltonic reminiscences here are quite obvious, and Tennyson's admiration for those simple mountain people who had
struggled so long against tyranny to keep their faith and freedom no doubt reminded him of Milton's indignant denunciation
of the Piedmontese who were successful in destroying the freedom of another rugged mountain people, the Waldensians. But
whereas the basic emotion of Milton's poem is indignation toward oppressors of truth and freedom, Tennyson's sonnet is
filled with enthusiasm for a small but dauntless people who have
succeeded in driving the forces of evil "in prone flight / By thou-
sands down the crags and thro' the vales." The earnest moral
tone, the plain, simple diction, the sense of the author's personal
involvement, combine to create a distinctly Miltonic mood, and
the meaning and emotion come through to the reader with only
the slightest assistance from poetic device. It is an extremely
effective sonnet, striking in its intensity and nobility.

The Victorians, of course, were struck by the similarity between the two sonnets, and it was the opinion of George Milner
that Tennyson "consciously matched himself against his great
predecessor." Recognizing that "Montenegro" was "of the highest quality," Milner noted that Tennyson's sonnet was closer to

the "orthodox" form than Milton's and that he had avoided
"the imperfection in the sestet" and had observed "the proper
division as to subject between the octave and sestet." "The English language," he concluded, "has no better instance of a
trumpet blast in fourteen lines than that which is furnished by
'Montenegro.'"[40]

Matthew Arnold, too, like Tennyson, had his moments of
liberalism in which he lashed out against the forces of oppression. His first sonnet, "To the Hungarian Nation," which appeared in *The Examiner* in 1849, is again in the "Piedmont"
tradition and heaps scorn on "that madhouse, France" and that
"American vulgarity." In anything but a disinterested mood,
Arnold cried:

> Hungarians! Save the world! Renew the stories
> Of men who against hope repell'd the chain,
> And make the world's dead spirit leap again!
> On land renew that Greek exploit, whose glories
> Hallow the Salaminian promontories,
> And the Armada flung to the fierce main.

Both Sanderlin and R. D. Havens believe that all of Arnold's
twenty-eight sonnets are Miltonic. In fact, Sanderlin says they
are "the most Miltonic poems since Wordsworth's Liberty
series." But both men find the strongest similarity in their spirit
and subject-matter: both Milton and Arnold "were classical,
resolute, scholarly; and these attributes were reflected in the
sonnets of each—classically exemplified in Arnold's 'To a
Friend.'"[41] Unfortunately, Milton's "What supports me, dost
thou ask?"[42] must have been the original of that bad first line
of an otherwise beautiful sonnet, "Who prop, thou ask'st, in
these bad days, my mind?"

Dante Rossetti, oddly enough, had little to do with Milton
and rarely mentioned him or his work. Perhaps Albert M.
Turner is right when he says: "It is astonishing at first sight
that Rossetti has passed over the august epics of Milton; our
wonder, however, ceases when we reflect that Milton's austere
grandeur must have been alien to Rossetti's warm southern

nature, but that his sonnets appealed because Rossetti too was a master of this form."[43] And perhaps Rossetti shared his sister's opinion which she stated in an unpublished letter, "Milton I cannot warm towards, even let alone all theological questions."[44] Nevertheless, Rossetti did respect Milton's sonnets, for Hall Caine quoted him as saying that Milton's sonnets "seem to me to be every one of them of exceptional excellence."[45] Furthermore, Rossetti, who seldom exhibited any interest in the political sphere, wrote two sonnets in the Miltonic mood during the late 1840's. In the sonnet "At the Sunrise in 1848," Rossetti celebrated the liberal uprisings on the Continent and hoped that a new day of freedom was dawning upon the earth. Again, the poetry of statement and the tone of righteous indignation are found in the sonnet of 1849, "On Refusal of Aid between Nations."

The appearance of Elizabeth Barrett Browning's *Sonnets from the Portuguese* in 1850 marks the beginning of a turn away from the dominant Miltonic pattern and a return in part to the Italian and Elizabethan sonnet writers in style and theme. But although this trend was carried to its high point by Rossetti in *The House of Life* (a sonnet sequence in which the Latinate diction is often quite Miltonic), the Miltonic sonnet remained a popular form for both poets and the reading public.

After 1850 Swinburne was among those who continued to write political sonnets in the Miltonic key.[46] "The Burden of Austria," written in 1866, is one of several in a group entitled *Dirae* which catches the Miltonic note of denunciation, and, much later, his sonnet "On the Russian Persecution of the Jews" is in the same mood and style.

But perhaps the most striking imitation of the "Piedmont" sonnet after Tennyson's "Montenegro" is Oscar Wilde's "On the Massacre of the Christians in Bulgaria."

> Christ, dost Thou live indeed? or are Thy bones
> Still straitened in their rock-hewn sepulchre?
> And was Thy Rising only dreamed by her
> Whose love of Thee for all her sin atones?

For here the air is horrid with men's groans,
The priests who call upon Thy name are slain,
Dost Thou not hear the bitter wail of pain
From those whose children lie upon the stones?
Come down, O Son of God! incestuous gloom
Curtains the land, and through the starless night
Over Thy Cross the Crescent moon I see!
If Thou in very truth didst burst the tomb
Come down, O Son of Man! and show Thy might
Lest Mahomet be crowned instead of Thee!

Although the political and religious sonnets of the nineteenth century often show the effect of the form and mood of the Miltonic sonnet, there are several sonnets written during the Victorian period in which the subject matter of *Paradise Lost* is very much in evidence. For example, Tennyson's early sonnet "Salve Lux Renata" is Shakespearean in form but very Miltonic in diction and theme. Its obvious echoes of the invocation to Light of the third book of *Paradise Lost* are apparent at once:

Hail Light, another Time to mortal eyes
Issuing from behind the starry veil!
How gently morn steals from the misty skies,
Touching dim heights with sheeted radiance pale.
Pleased I behold, for to my inward sight
Within that dawn there dawns a mystery,
The shining marvel of another light,
On this auspicious day newborn to me.
Therefore, Oh Lord, whose effluence increate
Was Light from everlasting; who dost call,
Each several morn 'Let there be light' and strait
For a day's space the light is over all,
Grant to my dawn of joy a dawnlike strength
To lead up into day of summer length.[47]

Similarly, Meredith's famous "Lucifer in Starlight" in almost every detail is reminiscent of Satan's journey from hell through chaos to his first glimpse of "This pendant world" hanging by a golden chain from the ramparts of heaven.

> On a starred night Prince Lucifer uprose.
> Tired of his dark dominion, swung the fiend
> Above the rolling ball, in cloud part screened,
> Where sinners hugged their specter of repose.
> Poor prey to his hot fit of pride were those.
> And now upon his western wing he leaned,
> Now his huge bulk o'er Afric's sands careened,
> Now the black planet shadowed Arctic snows.
> Soaring through wider zones that pricked his scars
> With memory of the old revolt from Awe,
> He reached the middle height, and at the stars,
> Which are the brain of heaven, he looked, and sank.
> Around the ancient track marched, rank on rank,
> The army of unalterable law.

When Meredith described the cosmic sweep of Lucifer's flight far above the earth, now "o'er Afric's sands," now over "Arctic snows," he perhaps had in mind the spaciousness of Milton's universe and Satan's flight as he surveyed with greatest admiration "All this World at once."[48] In *Paradise Lost,* Satan, huge like a ship, spread "his Sail-broad Vans" and "then from Pole to Pole" he viewed in breadth the new-made world and like a vulture careened above his unsuspecting prey, while heaven serene in radiant light shone beyond the "Constellations thick" which danced in order and harmony to the tune of the heavenly spheres. Not only the imagery and situation but the diction and sentence structure of this sonnet are Miltonic.

The vitality and strength of the Miltonic sonnet in the later nineteenth century is further illustrated by the fact that Gerard Manley Hopkins began his career as a sonnet writer by imitating and adapting it. His first eight sonnets, written in 1865, show how carefully Hopkins had studied Milton's poems. The sonnets "Where art thou friend," "My love is lessen'd," "I must feed fancy," and "You see that I have come to passion's end," are Miltonic in structure;[49] and the theme and diction in "See how Spring opens with disabling cold" recall Milton's early sonnet "How soon hath time." The one purely Miltonic sonnet in Hopkins' canon, however, is "Thou art indeed just, Lord."

Thou are indeed just, Lord, if I contend
With thee; but, sir, so what I plead is just.
Why do sinners' ways prosper? and why must
Disappointment all I endeavour end?
    Wert thou my enemy, O thou my friend,
How wouldst thou worse, I wonder, than thou dost
Defeat, thwart me? Oh, the sots and thralls of lust
Do in spare hours more thrive than I that spend,
Sir, life upon thy cause. See, banks and brakes
Now, leaved how thick! laced they are again
With fretty chervil, look, and fresh wind shakes
Them; birds build—but not I build; no, but strain,
Time's eunuch, and not breed one work that wakes.
Mine, O thou lord of life, send my roots rain.

Here, as in Milton's "Piedmont," God is directly and earnestly addressed in a moment of emotional intensity reminiscent, too, of Donne. The Miltonic structure is apparent especially in Hopkins' constant use of enjambement, which is most effective here in the way the last line of the octave runs over into the middle of the first line of the sestet, but with the arresting insertion of "Sir," which abruptly breaks the easy flow and momentum of the sentence, and reminds one of Milton's abrupt "Forget not" at the beginning of line 5 in "Piedmont." The sestet, which like the "Piedmont" sonnet rhymes *cd, cd, cd,* ends with a single sentence which has the partial effect of a Shakespearean couplet in that it halts the movement of the poem before the end, and focuses attention upon a climactic statement which in a compressed and narrow compass tersely summarizes what has gone before: "Mine, O thou lord of life, send my roots rain" is as intense and moving in its own way as are Milton's one-sentence conclusions, "They also serve who only stand and wait," and "I wak'd, she fled, and day brought back my night."

Like Hopkins, his close friend Robert Bridges was also greatly influenced by Milton's poetry. Bridges consciously modelled his sonnets in *The Growth of Love* on Milton's, and Albert Guerard has found none "in which some Miltonic characteristic, such as grammatical inversion or suspension of narrative verb, does not occur."[50]

Since the Victorians considered Milton's sonnets to be the expression of his most intimate feelings, these poems of necessity had considerable effect on the Victorian image of Milton the man. On the whole, the image conveyed by the sonnets was salutary, although the tone of denunciation and indignation in "Piedmont," "I did but prompt the age," and the *Tetrachordon* sonnet reinforced the Victorian picture of a stern, unamiable Puritan. Nevertheless, the attitude of humble submission and the tone of wistful loneliness in the sonnet on his blindness and "Methought I saw my late espoused saint" did much to soften the hearts of the public toward the great poet. Certainly there is evidence to the effect that this latter poem, along with the Italian sonnets and especially the sonnet addressed to Lady Margaret Ley, effectively combatted the notion that Milton was a woman-hater who mistreated his wives and daughters. Furthermore, the sonnets of friendship to Henry Lawes, Henry Vane, and Cyriack Skinner, so warm and cordial in their tone, showed that Milton was capable of both enjoying and sustaining friendship.

There can be no doubt that Milton's "little pieces" had sufficient power to evoke praise and emulation during the nineteenth century, and Hazlitt effectively stated his century's opinion of the matter when he wrote that "there could not have been a greater mistake or a more august piece of criticism than to suppose that Milton only shone on great subjects."[51]

IV ☞ The Religious Epic and the Miltonic Sublime

The immortal wars which gods and angels wage,
Are they not shown in Milton's sacred page?
His strain will teach what numbers best belong
To themes celestial told in epic song.

—BYRON, *Hints from Horace*

I   ACTUALLY THERE was little direct imitation of Milton during the Victorian period; in terms of quality there was nothing comparable to Keats's *Hyperion*. Scattered indications of Milton's direct influence can be observed, for instance, in some of Tennyson's early experiments, such as "Armageddon," and in Matthew Arnold's "Sohrab and Rustum," but the only extensive evidence of close imitation is found in the sonnet, as we have seen, and in the religious epic which had a great vogue during the 1820's and 1830's.

In that period between the death of Byron in 1824 and the publication of Tennyson's volume of 1842, when religious fervor was at a high point perhaps for the last time in England, the appearance of an unusually large number of religious poems and epics should not be particularly puzzling to us. But why was so much of this poetry so obviously Miltonic? Of course, Milton was, at the time, unanimously considered the greatest writer of religious epic in English, and this in itself partially explains his attraction. Yet what precisely did the readers and authors of this poetry relish most in Milton's epics? It was their "sublimity."

Throughout the nineteenth century, two epithets, more than any others, were applied to Milton and his work, "sublime" and "puritan." The latter epithet I shall discuss in a later chapter; the former will be of particular interest here, for it is important to know exactly what John Wilson of *Blackwood's* meant when he said, "Why, Paradise Lost is, by the consent of all the civilised world, declared to be the grandest and most *sublime* poem that ever emanated from the mind of man, equally so in *conception* and *execution*. It embraces all that human beings can feel or comprehend of themselves, their origin, and their destiny."[1] How, for instance, did George Gilfillan expect his readers to interpret his statement that Milton's Satan was "the most *tremendous conception* in the compass of poetry —the *sublimest* creation of the mind of man"?[2] (Italics added.)

Actually the Romantics and Victorians alike rolled both the rhetorical or Longinian Sublime and the natural Sublime into one comprehensive meaning and therefore considered Milton a master of the Sublime in both of its senses. When George Meredith thought of Milton as the creator of an elevated, refined, somewhat ornate, rhetorically sublime style, he compared his poetry

> to some deep-chested organ whose grand inspiration,
> Serenely majestic in utterance, lofty and calm,
> Interprets to mortals with melody great as its burthen
> The mystical harmonies chiming for ever throughout the bright spheres.[3]

But it was Milton the poet of the natural Sublime, the Sublime which emanates from the contemplation of God and His attributes evident in the cosmic universe and in terrestrial Nature, that prompted Robert Montgomery, the author of *The Omnipresence of the Deity,* to exclaim:

> how deep he plunged
> Into the infinite sublime of thought,
> Flaming with visions of infernal glare!
> How high amid the alienated host
> Of warring angels, he could dare ascend,

Look on the lightnings of Almighty wrath,
Array the thunders, and reveal the God![4]

In short, when the Romantics and early Victorians spoke of
Milton as sublime, they usually meant both Sublimes; but it was
the natural Sublime amply exhibited in his epics which really
attracted and inspired English poets during the 1820's and
1830's.

The Longinian sublime, which was closely related to what
critics described as the "grand style," became increasingly important and prominent in England after Boileau's translation
of the *Peri Hupsous* of the pseudo-Longinus became known in
England after 1674, and concurrently, if not before, the native
English notion of the natural Sublime, the "Sublime in external
nature," as Marjorie Nicolson terms it, also attracted much attention and was defined by John Dennis in *The Grounds of
Criticism in Poetry* (1704) and described—but not so named—
by Joseph Addison in the series of *Spectator* papers on "The
Pleasures of the Imagination" (1712).[5]

Dennis believed that sublimity or "enthusiasm" comes from
the "Meditation of things that belong not to common life,"[6]
and that the enthusiastic passions such as admiration, terror,
horror, joy, sadness, and desire are caused by great objects and
particularly by "Divine Ideas" "which shew the Attributes or
relate to the Worship of Divinity."[7] For instance, "enthusiastic
Terror," which "contributes extremely to the Sublime" is, said
Dennis, produced by ideas of "Gods, Daemons, Hell, Spirits
and Souls of Men, Miracles, Prodigies, . . . Thunder, Tempests,
. . . Inundations, . . . Earthquakes, . . . Monsters, . . . Fires,
War, Pestilence, Famine, etc." But of all the ideas which cause
sublime emotions, "none are so terrible as those which shew
the Wrath and Vengeance of an angry God."[8]

Although Addison did not, like Dennis, stress the notion
that the source of the Sublime in Nature is the power and
wrath of an awesome God, he did believe that the pleasures of
the imagination come from "the Sight of what is Great, Un-
common, or Beautiful"; and by "greatness" he meant not only

"the Bulk of any single Object, but the Largeness of a whole View," especially those prospects which displayed the "stupendous Works of Nature" in their rude magnificence. "We are flung," he declared, "into a pleasing Astonishment" when our imagination attempts "to grasp at any thing that is too big for its Capacity."[9]

Both Dennis and Addison, then, were attracted to *Paradise Lost* not only because of the Longinian Sublime in its style and diction but also for the abundant evidence of the natural Sublime. In fact, John Dennis was so impressed with Milton's cosmic scenes and titanic beings that he used *Paradise Lost,* "the greatest Poem that ever was written by Man," as the chief illustration of the Sublime in *The Grounds of Criticism.*[10]

This interest in the natural Sublime increased rapidly during the eighteenth century, became an important element in the Romantic Movement, and continued to be a potent force in the literature and life of the early Victorians. Just as the true source of the Sublime was, for Dennis, in religion and the contemplation of the Deity and His vast, limitless creation, so was it for a large and influential segment of Victorian society. Nothing pleased the early Victorians more than paintings, sermons, and poetry which freed their minds from restraint and lifted them to a state of emotional transcendence. As a result, canvases, books, and sermons were filled with direct appeals to the visual imagination designed to arouse sublime feelings. Since the Sublime was the result of contemplating great things, beginning with the terror and admiration that came from seeing the power of God manifesting itself in the universe, artists and poets crammed their works with enormous objects and panoramas, limitless space, vast and irregular landscapes, titanic beings, and cataclysmic occurrences. The Bible was ransacked for sublime subjects, especially catastrophes, such as the Deluge, the fall of Nineveh, the Millennium, and the Last Judgment.

If a poet, artist, or preacher catered to the public's desire for the Sublime, he suddenly found himself the center of great enthusiasm and adulation. For instance, the secret of success for Edward Irving—the most popular preacher of his day—a fiery young Scotsman who came to London in 1822 as pastor of a small, dingy chapel in Holborn, was his "sublimity." Increasingly eccentric and mystical in his preaching, Irving filled his audience with Dennis' "enthusiastic passions" of terror and admiration when he prophesied the destruction of the wicked and described in the most vivid, forceful language the end of time and the last judgment. To be horrified, awe-stricken, or entertained, tremendous, crushing crowds descended on the Hatton Garden chapel Sunday after Sunday and willingly paid a guinea and a half to push inside to hear the sermon. Appealing to all types and classes of people, Irving numbered among his frequent auditors Canning, Peel, De Quincey, Coleridge, Carlyle, Macaulay, Jeremy Bentham, William Godwin, and hosts of others.[11] In 1828, on a visit to Edinburgh, the preacher filled to overflowing the city's largest church day after day; the drawing card: a series of sermons on the Apocalypse, delivered at six o'clock in the morning. Later in the year at Perth, while Irving was preaching on the coming of the Son of Man, a dark cloud descended upon the neighborhood and covered the church in ominous shade. Suddenly the air was rent by a great explosion of thunder and the flash of lightning. "There was deep stillness in the congregation. The preacher paused; then from the stillness and the gloom his powerful voice rang out: 'For as the lightning cometh out of the east, and shineth even unto the west, so shall the coming of the Son of Man be.' "[12] The effect, to say the least, was sublime.

But Milton's *Paradise Lost,* too, was sublime; its subject was sublime, its setting was sublime, and its chief character, Satan, was sublime. The subject of the epic was God and the justification of his ways to man; the setting was the whole cosmic universe—hell, earth, and heaven; and the chief character was a superhuman being who dared to think the most terrifying thoughts and to attempt the most awful deeds imaginable. And because the natural Sublime was so prominent in *Paradise Lost,* the would-be writers of religious epics naturally turned to Milton for guidance.

A whole group of now-forgotten poets such as Robert Pollok, Robert Montgomery, John Abraham Heraud, Edwin Atherstone, William Phillips, Edward Reade, and others, gained a phenomenal popularity by writing religious epic poetry. They, like Milton, took the whole universe for their setting, and chose God and his angels, and Satan with his legions for their *dramatis personae.* Oftentimes the design of these poems differed from that of *Paradise Lost* only in the greater comprehensiveness and vastness of the plan. Indeed, what one reviewer said of Robert Montgomery's *Messiah* applies generally to all: these poems attempt to relate to us "not only the world made, and the world lost, but the world regained; and, in the meantime, the history of all occurrences—the deeds and doings of all the Prophets, good and evil."[13] What Professor Stoll once said of Milton might also be applied to these poets, for it describes the elements in Milton which impressed them: "Space is indispensable to him, and he takes to 'Pisgah-visions' far and wide, from province to province. He delights in what is vague and vast, dim and shadowy, immense and mysterious."[14] Predominantly Miltonic, the quality of these poems is at times modified by aspects of Goethe's *Faust* and Dante's *Divine Comedy,* and the authors no doubt were also familiar with Blake's later poetry and the Byron of *Manfred* and *Cain.*

Whatever the ancestry might have been, the religious epic satisfied the early Victorian taste for flamboyant religious literature in a rather extraordinary but extremely successful way. In a period of revived evangelicalism, the poetry of Milton was highly acceptable and popular because of its religious subject matter; and, as a result, a number of popular painters as well as the poets turned to Milton for inspiration in their attempt to be sublime.

It is interesting to note how closely the apocalyptic school of artists such as Henry Fuseli and John Martin parallels what could be called the apocalyptic school of poets in the 1820's and 1830's. Often there was a close interconnection between these two groups, not only because they drew a great deal of their inspiration from Milton, but because they oftentimes aimed at winning popularity through the exploitation of the public's desire for religious themes in art surrounded and heightened by highly imaginative settings.

John Martin (1789–1854),[15] perhaps the most typical apocalyptic painter, collaborated on several occasions with the apocalyptic poets,[16] and his Milton designs are approvingly discussed by Satan in Robert Montgomery's popular poem entitled *Satan*. Gazing with admiration at Martin's painting which depicts the expulsion of the rebel angels, the Fiend declares:

> The midnight and immensity of art
> I see; as though his eye had seen the hour
> When down in thunder through the yawning skies
> A whirlwind of rebellious angels came!—
> The painter hath infernal pomp reveal'd
> That second Milton, whose creative soul
> Doth shadow visions to such awful life,
> That men behold them with suspended breath
> And grow ethereal at a gaze. . . .
>
> (p. 344)

Martin, who by the 1830's had gained tremendous popularity and international fame,[17] had painted canvases as early as 1813 depicting Miltonic subjects such as *Adam's First Sight of Eve* and *The Expulsion of Adam and Eve*. His *Belshazzar's Feast* of 1821 won him a prize of two hundred pounds at the British Institution, and later he received the handsome sum of two thousand pounds for drawing and engraving a fine series of twenty-four mezzotints of *Paradise Lost*.

These engravings, which appeared in numerous editions of the epic until the plates literally wore out, represent Martin's best work.[18] They were executed between 1825 and 1827 and were dedicated to King George IV. The prospectus speaks of "the lofty undertaking of embodying the stupendous and preternatural imagery of the *Paradise Lost;* in which the sublime genius of *Milton* has given those wonderful descriptions of *Heaven*, and *Hell*, and *Paradise*, and *Chaos*, and *Creation*." Heretofore, *Paradise Lost* has not "been treated with a boldness and grandeur kindred to the mighty imagination which created [it]."[19]

But Martin was only one of several artists who imitated Henry Fuseli,[20] a brilliant painter of daring invention, who—long before the Pre-Raphaelites—delighted to find his themes in poetry, especially that of Milton, Dante, and Shakespeare. Frederick Antal notes that Fuseli particularly favored poetry "of an imaginative or visionary character." He searched increasingly in Milton, Shakespeare, and Gray "for terrifying, breathtaking scenes at their highest moment of tension, where the violent passions of forceful personalities could be portrayed."[21]

Fuseli was a friend of Blake and the only contemporary artist whom Blake admired. Each influenced the other, but it is Antal's opinion that "Blake was more under Fuseli's influence than the other way around."[22] In 1799 Fuseli exhibited a series of paintings from subjects furnished by Milton's works which he hoped would form a Milton gallery corresponding to Boydell's Shakespeare Gallery. His paintings of *Sin coming between Satan and Death* (based on *Paradise Lost,* II, 722 ff.) and *The Vision of the Madhouse* (based on *Paradise Lost,* XI, 477 ff.) from this collection show striking resemblance to Blake's illustrations of Milton's epic.[23]

Robert Pollok's epic, *The Course of Time,* illustrates the influence of the apocalyptic painters upon the poets in a rather interesting way when, instead of directly describing the conflagration of the earth at the end of time, Pollok displayed it as an apocalyptic painting on the walls of the New Jerusalem:

> look, and behold,
> On spacious canvas, touched with living hues,—
> The Conflagration of the ancient earth,
> The handiwork of high arch-angel, drawn
> From memory of what he saw that day.
> See how the mountains, how the valleys burn!
> The Andes burn, the Alps, the Appennines;
> Taurus and Atlas, all the islands burn;
> The Ocean burns, and rolls his waves of flame.
> See how the lightnings, barbed, red with wrath,

Sent from the quiver of Omnipotence,
Cross and recross the fiery gloom, and burn
Into the centre![24]

Recently, Kitson Clark referred in passing to Milton's relationship to the apocalyptic painters and the writers of religious
epics when he said that "most unfortunately" Milton "probably
suggested the poems on large scale religious subjects very like
what the public demanded from the apocalyptic painters, as
when Thomas Ragg, a working man, wrote an epic in twelve
books on *The Deity,* or William Ellis Wall, an M.A. of Trinity College, Oxford, wrote another, also in twelve books, on
Christ Crucified."[25]

II   Thus it was during the late 1820's, when
John Martin's apocalyptic paintings and Edward Irving's sublime sermons were taking the English by
storm, that the group of "apocalyptic" poets and their religious
epics made their appearance and also gained extraordinary popularity. It is difficult to believe that at one time they almost
completely monopolized the attention of the critics as well as
the public, and were denounced and praised in the most extravagant terms imaginable. Although these poets had their admirers among the critics, the major reviewers, John Wilson,
William Maginn, and Thomas Macaulay, were extremely hostile.

Certainly none of the apocalyptic poets ever aroused and provoked the reviewers as did Robert Montgomery, the "chief specimen" of a "modern school of verse, (which seeks not less
than to supplant the poetry of Milton)."[26] In 1827 at the age
of twenty he published his first Miltonic imitation, called "The
Crucifixion," and the following year came "A Vision of Heav-
en" and "A Vision of Hell." But soon afterwards, his poem
The Omnipresence of the Deity (not Miltonic in form) satisfied the popular religious sentiment so exactly that it ran
through eight editions in as many months. This poem and another, entitled *Satan,* called forth two vicious articles by Wil-

liam Maginn in *Fraser's Magazine*,[27] and a particularly scathing attack by Macaulay in the *Edinburgh Review*.[28] Both Macaulay and Maginn were concerned and irritated by the fact that the reading public (whom they reviled for being dupes) could be so misled by such "trash," and, consequently, they accused Montgomery and his publisher of taking malicious advantage of the public's zealous desire for religious reading material. For instance, it was hard for Maginn to understand how "the herd of wonder-stricken jackasses amongst the devout and the ignorant, vociferate *papae!* and wonderful! and astonishing boy! and surpassing sanctity!"[29] And after a detailed mauling of *The Omnipresence of the Deity* and choice remarks on *Satan,* Macaulay, in his review of the poems, summed up the contents of *Satan* in a satirical blaze and referred slightingly to John Martin's appearance in the poem:[30]

> *Satan* is a long soliloquy, which the Devil pronounces in five or six thousand lines of blank verse, concerning geography, politics, newspapers, fashionable society, theatrical amusements, Sir Walter Scott's novels, Lord Byron's poetry, and Mr. Martin's pictures. The new designs for Milton have, as was natural, particularly attracted the attention of a personage who occupies so conspicuous a place in them. Mr. Martin must be pleased to learn, that, whatever may be thought of those performances on earth, they give full satisfaction in Pandemonium, and that he is there thought to have hit off the likenesses of the various Thrones and Dominations very happily.[31]

The reviewer for the *Athenaeum,* too, was unable to account for the great success of Montgomery's poetry. *Satan,* he said, is "the utmost trial of the taste of that numerous class of persons who bought and believed in the 'Omnipresence of the Deity,' . . . The only ground which it is possible to fancy any one would take for praising this poem is its high tone of moral and religious pretension." Summarizing the situation, the reviewer wrote:

> All appear in him to be mere sounding words, used for the sake of persuading himself and others that his mind is occupied on high subjects, of being the idol of tea-tables, and of selling nine editions

of his poems. . . . He has meddled with nothing but the dead and empty words; and with them he has constructed popular volumes, and made himself a name which is great today among the professors of religion, literature, and all uncharitableness, and which will assuredly be to-morrow as completely forgotten as that of any other detected saltimbanco.[32]

In April, 1830, William Maginn produced a second article on the writers of religious epics in which he castigated Montgomery for a page or so, went on to praise a new poem by John Abraham Heraud, and concluded by ridiculing another by William Phillips. Maginn noted with disgust that since the appearance of his first article, the printer of *Satan* had not "Shut up his own shop in utter dismay and despair," and had continued to sell this "religious trash" to "devout fools" who "flocked to his counter to purchase it." Worst of all, the popular demand had tempted other "rhythm-essayists" to try their hand at "sundry poems, of ample thickness and balsam weight, to wit, *Creation, Mount Sinai, The Impious Feast, Cain,* etc."[33]

Next, however, Maginn turned his attention to "one green and verdant island" among all this waste, *The Descent into Hell,* which he praised because it was based upon "the only two models worthy of observance," *Paradise Lost* and *The Divine Comedy.*[34] To be sure, the poem differs from the other apocalyptic poems in one respect: despite its Miltonic style, its measure is the *terza rima* of Dante. The poem was published anonymously in 1830 and received this high praise from Maginn not really because it differed in quality and type from the others of its class, but because the author was John Abraham Heraud, the associate of Maginn in the new *Fraser's Magazine.* Finally Maginn directed the reader's attention away from *The Descent* to "the gesticulations of an ape" and the consideration of yet another religious epic, *Mount Sinai,* by a Mr. William Phillips. After citing numerous passages in the poem which were paraphrases and direct imitations of similar passages in *Paradise Lost,* Maginn concluded, "Milton run stark staring mad, would be too gentle a term for this gentleman's performance."[35]

The same month in which Maginn's review of *Satan* appeared, John Wilson in an anonymous article reviewed Edwin Atherstone's *The Fall of Nineveh*.[36] Wilson, too, was anything but pleased with the deluge of apocalyptic art, and wondered if its stupidity might not be contagious: "The truth is, we have read Mr. Atherstone till we have become almost—you would not believe us, did we say wholly—as stupid as himself."[37] The reviewer was at pains throughout to convict Atherstone of outright plagiarism: "Mr. Atherstone is a most ambitious mimic. For, besides catching the trick of Byron, he takes off—who do you think?—Homer and Milton!"[38] Wilson dwelt at length on Atherstone's paraphrases of Milton's *Paradise Lost,* and in one instance quoted the poet's long invocation in its entirety and then addressed him: "That is by no means badly expressed; and had you been one of the Great Poets, the Invocation would have been rather a little or so sublime. But unluckily you are no poet at all—and the passage, though you have taken care to alter all or most of the words, is the property of a blind man, one John Milton. You think you are writing poetry, while you are only playing at cribbage."[39]

Next Wilson attacked another essential element of the religious epic, the long, seemingly endless geographical descriptions. Milton, he said, "sweeps the earth with an angel's wing, from the regions of the rising to the regions of the setting sun—shewing you in one panorama, it may almost be said, the whole habitable globe. Mr. Atherstone, too, must needs be topographical and geographical; but he has not even the merit of a land-measurer, and merely mouths out so many names from the gazetteer."[40] Without doubt, Atherstone, like his fellow apocalyptics, often wrote his poems with "a description by Milton in one eye" and "his own Vision" in the other.

In many ways, the most important critical essay which deals with the writers of religious epic is an anonymous review of Edmund Reade's *Cain the Wanderer* and *The Revolt of the Angels* and *The Fall from Paradise*.[41] Here the author reviewed the status of poetry in 1830, and like so many of his fellow critics he found the situation rather depressing. He was led to believe that the "spirit of the age is not eminently favourable to poetry,"[42] because, as he wrote, we nowadays "turn to prose for information; from poetry we require that it shall interest our feelings, and excite our imagination."[43] Thus there was less need for a great quantity of poetry but more need for poetry "of the highest stamp." The reviewer noticed a change "from tame and didactic, to poetry the most stirring, romantic, and impassioned." This was as it should be, but these qualities could be and were being carried too far by some poets. We now encounter

> eccentricity and exaggeration,—a false and feverish view of nature, —a proneness to mystify and distort,—a proneness, also, to travel out of the homely "working-day world,"—to pass even the bounds of time and space in search of themes. One of the principal characteristics of the poetry of the last few years is, its choice of subjects, with which none but the mightiest genius could effectively grapple. . . . Pictures of other states of being are now familiarly set before us; we have Visions of Heaven, of Hell, and of Creation. The Revolt of the Angels, and the Field of Armageddon, must help us to beguile the listlessness of a vacant hour; half-fledged poets . . . adopt for their hero "Satan," and talk as familiarly of the "crack of doom," "as maids of fifteen do of puppy dogs."[44]

Mr. Reade is just such a poet, said the critic, and he "has boldly measured his strength against Milton and Byron"; indeed, a "new survey of the ground which we thought had been left to Milton, is presented in Mr. Reade's second publication, wherein we find the 'Revolt of the Angels,' and the 'Fall from Paradise.' "[45] In this discussion, the apocalyptic poets are described very well, and it is because Milton's poetry passed "even the bounds of time and space" and dealt with the superhuman and mystic that the public and these poets and artists preferred to imitate him rather than, say, Shakespeare.[46]

III   John Wilson, *Blackwood's* Christopher North, was talking about the Sublime in nature when he said that Milton's "Heavenly Muse, in Heaven,

is God's thought of the Beauty which shall be in the Universe
to be created," and that the "Heavenly Muse upon Earth is the
Human Sense of Beauty" or the sense within the human soul
capable of recognizing and responding emotionally to the Sublime, "God's thought of Beauty" in the universe. Moreover,
Wilson's "capacious meaning" of Beauty makes even more evident the fact that he was thinking in terms of the Sublime, for
it includes "the solemn, the sublime" and any other qualities
which "affect the mind suddenly, and without time given for
reflection," and that appear "as a glory poured over . . . the
natural universe." Wilson's belief that the Beautiful or Sublime
in nature "affects us with irreflective admiration—appears as
a glory—stupendous forests—mountains—rivers—the solemn,
boundless munificence of the starry firmament," was a belief
held firmly by those writers who were attracted to the Sublime
in Milton's epics and who attempted to imitate him in their
own poems.[47]

The "stupendous" in nature, the "boundless munificence" of
creation, the vast and great wherever found—these produced
the desired effect in literature: Sublimity; and this induced the
desired effect in the reader: emotional tension and a heightened
awareness of a tremendous, terrifying force at work in the universe. In his preface to *The Judgement of the Flood,* John Abraham Heraud not only described the "spirit and contents" of his
epic, but also predicted the desired effect on his readers when
he wrote: "all is purposely gigantick,—the plot—the persons
—the crimes—the language, and the imagery. After the perusal
of such a work, if adequately executed, one ought to feel as if
just emerged from an apparently illimitable cathedral, cut out
by the hand of nature in the recesses of an alpine region,
equally remarkable for loftiness of elevation and extent of
area."[48]

Naturally any book, religious or scientific, which described
great events and vast scenes was eagerly sought out by the
writers of religious epics in the 1820's and 1830's. The Bible,
with its magnificent descriptions of creation, the Deluge, heroic

warriors and divine prophets, was an important source for plots and inspiration, especially the Book of Revelation with its apocalyptic descriptions of such sublime events as the Millennium, the war between God and Satan, the conflagration, and the Last Judgment. The Book of Revelation was not only a source for Milton and the Apocalyptics but it was also a model of great religious poetry. Dr. Johnson's idea "that sacred subjects are unfit for poetry" was, in fact, refuted by a reviewer of Thomas Ragg's *The Deity* who pointed out "that a considerable portion of the volume of Revelation *is* poetry—poetry of the sublimest kind."[49]

During the earlier eighteenth century, as Marjorie Nicolson has shown, Milton's *Paradise Lost* and Thomas Burnet's *The Sacred Theory of the Earth* "were the two most widely read theodicies," and these two authors "were more responsible than any other English writers for the cult of literary sublimity."[50] It is interesting to note that during the nineteenth century both works were still inspiring the authors of the Sublime even though Milton's epic had far outdistanced its nearest competitor. A letter of 1821 from the Poet Laureate, Robert Southey, to his protégé John Heraud indicates that great subjects such as the Deluge and great books like *The Sacred Theory* were still commanding consideration. Heraud, who had been considering the Flood as the subject of an epic, had written for advice to Southey who replied:

> The Deluge is a noble subject for which I formed a plan drawn from the state of the present world, and to have been executed in hexameters as far back as the year 1799. You will be struck by this coincidence. That plan is laid aside for ever, my race as a poet being nearly run. I meant to have adopted Burnet's 'Theory of the Earth,' and recommend it to you. If it should not please you for your purpose it will in other respects, as being one of the sublimest works of imagination.[51]

But for the nineteenth-century worshipers of the vast, remote, and the terrible, Milton's epics, *Paradise Lost* and *Paradise Regained,* suggested suitable plots, settings, characters, diction, versification, and inspiration. What attracted them most were the Miltonic universe, where the Sublime in God, space, and terrestrial Nature was clearly evident, and the Miltonic Satan, the grandest, most sublime figure in all literature.

The Miltonic universe—its heaven above and hell far below with the earth and chaos and myriads of worlds in between— was congenial to a mind which, as Addison said, "naturally hates everything that looks like a Restraint upon it";[52] and certainly it was appealing to the poet who, "disdainful of material bounds, / In spiritual romance delights to dream."[53] But, of course, we are talking here about "modern" man, Spengler's "Faustian" man, whose thirst for experience brooks no restraint, the "modern" man as opposed to the "ancient" in the writings of Schiller. And it is precisely the "modern" element in Milton's epics—the response to the vast and limitless, the "Faustian" element in Satan—which renders them more attractive and satisfying to the apocalyptic poets and artists than the Greek spirit of calm simplicity and joy in the common things of life found in the epics of Homer. Edwin Atherstone made this perfectly clear when in *The Fall of Nineveh* he invoked that "Great Spirit" who supported Homer, "yet favour'd more," Milton, who sang to the solemn harp about "Paradise, Chaos, and Heaven and Hell, in verse sublime."[54]

The setting of Robert Pollok's epic, *The Course of Time* (1827), exhibits the Miltonic universe in all its sublimity. That he like Milton was aesthetically responsive to the vast and infinite is apparent throughout the ten books. Seeking the Sublime at its fountain-head, the epic opens with a description of heaven where "Mountains of tallest stature circumscribe / The plains of Paradise." Far above "in middle heaven remote" is seen "the mount of God in awful glory bright."

Pollok's heaven, like Milton's, is surrounded by "battlements" from which one can delight to behold

ten thousand worlds
Around their suns revolving in the vast

> Eternal space, or listen [to] the harmonies
> That each to other in is motion sings.
>
> (Vol. I, p. 13)

But "beyond the visible creation," past the bounds

> Which God doth set to light and life and love;
> Where darkness meets with day, where order meets
> Disorder dreadful, waste and wild; and down
> The dark, eternal, uncreated night,

there are

> empty, nameless regions vast,
> Where utter Nothing dwells, unformed and void,

and this leads downward to

> . . . unclaimed continents of desert gloom
> Immense, where gravitation shifting turns
> The other way.
>
> (Vol. I, pp. 18–19)

Farther still yawns the gate of hell guarded by Sin and "undescribed" Death, and within lie the vast, illimitable lakes and continents of the burning underworld of eternal punishment.

The enthusiastic passions of admiration and terror are fully evident in this epic. For when God's voice is heard declaring the end of time (Vol. II, pp. 233 ff.),

> all the Sacred Hill on high
> Burned, terrible with glory, and, behind
> The uncreated lustre, hid the Lamb,
> Invisible.

Then the Son, "divine similitude! Image express of Deity unseen!" in majestic procession goes forth to the Last Judgment, a scene which should be compared with Milton's description of the Son's procession into Chaos to create the world (*Paradise Lost,* VII, 192–231):

> And now the Trump of wondrous melody,
> By man or angel never heard before,
> Sounded with thunder, and the march began.

The Son armed with the book of God's remembrance, and his sword of "justice ultimate,"

> Not swift, as cavalcade, on battle bent,
> But, as became procession of a judge,
> Solemn, magnificent, majestic, slow;
> Moving sublime with glory infinite,
> And numbers infinite, and awful song,
> They passed the gate of heaven, which many a league,
> Opened either way, to let the glory forth
> Of this great march.

(Vol. II, p. 243)

After the judgment has been pronounced and the good and faithful wafted into heaven,

> God grew dark with utter wrath;
> And drawing now the sword, undrawn before,
> Which through the range of infinite, all round,
> A gleam of fiery indignation threw,
> He lifted up his hand omnipotent,
> And down among the damned the burning edge
> Plunged; . . .
>
> .   .   .   .
>
> They howling fled to west among the dark;
> But fled not these the terrors of the Lord;
> Pursued, and driven beyond the Gulph, which frowns
> Impassable, between the good and bad,
> And downward far remote to left, oppressed
> And scorched with the avenging fires, begun
> Burning within them,—they upon the verge
> Of Erebus, a moment, pausing stood,
> And saw, below, the unfathomable lake,
> Tossing with tides of dark, tempestuous wrath;
> And would have looked behind; but greater wrath,
> Behind, forbade, which now no respite gave
> To final misery: God, in the grasp
> Of his Almighty strength, took them upraised,
> And threw them down, into the yawning pit
> Of bottomless perdition, ruined, damned,
> Fast bound in chains of darkness evermore.

(Vol. II, pp. 248–49)

Similarly, in the religious poetry of Robert Montgomery, the Miltonic universe becomes "one vast temple . . . where shadows of his [God's] glory are enshrined." Vast cosmic perspectives open before us in "A Vision of Heaven" as the poet tells how once "disembodied" his spirit soared upward through the air like a bird,

> Till Earth beneath me in the glassy depth
> Lay twinkling like a star; but all around,
> Those burning mysteries that mortals glance
> With wonder, floating o'er the face of night,
> Not drops of fire, but full and perfect worlds,
> In congregations vast as glorious,—beam'd.[55]

But Montgomery in *The Omnipresence of the Deity* (1828) chose to describe the wonder and sublimity of God in this world. "There is a voiceless eloquence on Earth," he declared, which tells "of Him who gave her wonders birth";

> And long may I remain the adoring child
> Of Nature's majesty, sublime or wild;
> Hill, flood, and forest, mountain, rock, and sea,
> *All take their terrors and their charms from Thee,*
> From Thee, whose hidden but supreme control
> Moves through the world, a universal soul.[56]

(Italics added.)

The terrestrial Sublime, however, is best exhibited in these religious epics when the poets closely imitate the scenes in *Paradise Regained* where Satan takes the Son of God "up to a Mountain high," and by use of his "Aery Microscope" shows Him the vast stretches of the earth and all its fabulous kingdoms.[57] In Montgomery's *Messiah,* Book Four describes the temptations of Christ in the wilderness. First the natural Sublime is displayed in a great storm (cf. *Paradise Regained,* IV, 409–425) which sweeps over the desert waste and breaks above the head of the Messiah:

> But when hath tempest, since a deluge roar'd,
> The pale earth shaken, like that stormy rage

That tore the desert, while Messiah mused?
Then God to hands infernal seem'd to trust
The helm of Nature, while a chaos drove
The elements to combat!—night and storm,
And rain and whirlwind, in their frenzied wrath
Triumphant, while aloft unnat'ral clouds
Hung o'er the sky the imag'ry of Hell!—
Not hence alone tempestuous horror sprung:
To aid the Tempter, shapes of ghastly light,
With phantoms, grim beyond a maniac's dream,
To thunder, darkness, and dread midnight gave
A power unearthly:—round thy sleepless head,
Adored Redeemer! did the voices chant,
Or wildly mutter their unhallow'd spell;
Yet all serene Thy godlike virtue stood,—
Unshaken, though the universe might fall![58]

Then Satan, "swiftly by an airy flight," takes Messiah "To Quarantania's unascended top / That crowns the Wilderness with savage pomp" where they see spread before them a sublime view of the world which is obviously modelled after similar scenes in *Paradise Regained* (cf. III, 251 ff. and especially IV, 25–60). From the top of the mountain

                    a world
In visionary light lay all revealed
With luring splendour!—regions, thrones and climes
Of bloom and fragrance, meadows, lakes, and groves:
And there lay cities, capp'd with haughty towers,
With piles, and palaces of marble sheen,
And domes colossal, with exalting flags
Of royal conquest on their gilded spires:
And there were armies, thick as trooping clouds,
On plains assembled,—chariot, smoke, and steed,
The pomp of death, and thunder—gloom of war!
Nor absent, fleets within the silver bay
Reposed, or riding o'er a gallant sea:
All this, the world's inspirer thus evoked,—
One vast enchantment, one enormous scene
Of splendour, deluging the dazzled eye
With mingled radiance, till the fancy reel'd!

                                        (p. 107)

Montgomery, "that soaring Miltonic genius," was, indeed,
fond of these sublime panoramas, and included other vast
scenes reminiscent of *Paradise Regained* in his *Satan*. In this
epic of which a reviewer said that the poet "urges his Pegasus
far beyond the limits of time and space, and holds converse
with spirits of every degree,"[59] Montgomery used Milton's line
"Earth's Kingdoms and their glory" for his epigraph. Then he
revealed Satan standing alone on a mountain peak buffeted by
fierce tempests:

> Awake, ye thunders! let your living roar
> Exult around me, and a darkness shroud
> The air, as once again the world I greet,
> Here on this haughty mountain-head, where He
> Of old, now palaced in the Heaven of Heavens,
> The Virgin-born, by Prophets vision'd both,
> Was tempted, and withstood me!
>
> (p. 19)

When the storm clears, Satan looks at the sun and sees the glory
of God reflected there:

> The Sun is up! look, where he proudly comes,
> In blazing triumph wheeling o'er the earth,
> A victor in full glory! At his gaze
> The heavens magnificently smile, . . .
>   . . . Yes, land, and air
> Whose winged fulness freshens tree and flower,
> Own thee, thou shining Monarch of the skies!
>
> (p. 23)

In this poem, which "abounds in passages of beauty and sublimity, which have few parallels in modern times,"[60] Satan sees

> A mass of kingdoms, continents, and isles!
> Oceans,—those royal elements, outspread,
> Heaving and wild, monotonously vast!
> Terrific mountains, where the fire floods dwell,
> Or snows in cold eternity congeal;
> And haggard rocks uplifted, huge and bare,
> The hoary frame-work of a ruined world; . . .
> Before me, like a panorama, spread!

> Wherever Earth by Nature's seal is stamp'd,
> Far as the ice-clad North hath bared her brow,
> To where the burning South extends—from East
> To West, the theatre of Man I view.
>
> (pp. 24–25)

Later, his "vision spanning the world," Satan describes another vast terrestrial scene:

> Lo, in the East! enormously uprear'd
> What ice-peak'd mountains point their roseate heads
> Amid the richness of their Indian sky,
> Soundless and solemn, as cathedral towers
> Made dim and spectral by the wintry moon.
> Hills of the North! not all your Greenland pomp
> Can more sublimely scale the clouds. And where,
> O Ganges! mountain-born, careers the flood
> That watches thee?
>
> (p. 51)

By filling their epics with such passages, which at least superficially fit the definition of the Sublime in Nature, Montgomery and his fellow poets sought to arouse great emotions in their readers. Attempting to imitate Milton's sublimity, they combined the Longinian Sublime with both aspects of the natural Sublime—the terrible and awsome power of God and its manifestation in natural objects and elements. But potent as the formula was, the genius, artistry, and inspiration of Milton were totally lacking. Nevertheless, many like Isaac Taylor evidently believed that they succeeded rather well, for in his Introductory Essay to Thomas Ragg's *The Deity* (1834), he remarked that religious poets such as Ragg could come closer to discovering and exhibiting the essential qualities of God than even the best philosophers because "the combination of the reasoning faculty with imaginative tastes and the poetic sentiment peculiarly favours the apprehension of those sublime doctrines wherein the highest abstractions are intimately blended with conceptions of vastness, harmony, felicity, and goodness."[61]

IV   If the grandeur and spaciousness of the Miltonic universe were congenial to the apocalyptic poets and their public, the Miltonic Satan was equally appealing. Furthermore, there were two qualities above all others which attracted them to Satan. First, he was a sublime being; that is, Milton in creating him "combined in one stupendous figure every species of beauty, deformity, terror, darkness, light, calm, convulsion—the essence of man, devil, and angel, collected into a something distinct from each, and absolutely unique."[62] Secondly, Satan, now freed from his tail, hoofs, and horns, had become a human being with god-like qualities, or a hero, a "faded god" demoted to human status. And, as a result, he exhibited those human characteristics—pride, unconquerable will, ambition, bravery, pity, and remorse—which, more than any others, call forth the sympathetic understanding of other human beings. As Shelley saw it, Satan was the victim of "misery and injustice" which invariably "contrive to produce very poetical effects, because the excellence of poetry consists in its awakening the sympathy of men."[63] Therefore, Satan was the hero of *Paradise Lost*—"the most interesting character," "the most heroic subject that ever was chosen for a poem"—because he was a sublime and sympathetic being.

Sublimity, as I have said, is characterized by "greatness" which in proportion to its magnitude arouses the passions, especially feelings of terror and admiration. A gigantic mountain is sublime because it is physically huge, but Satan was sublime not only because he was physically as tremendous and terrifying as Leviathan, but also because he was intellectually a titan whose thoughts and aims were as great as his physical stature. "His strength of mind," said Hazlitt, "was matchless as his strength of body."[64] Satan is a "colossal figure," Masson remarked, but his "greatness lies in the vastness of his motives."[65]

Like Faust whose aspiring mind scorned the life of inaction and impotence, and strove to "o'er leap" all bounds in his bid for knowledge and power, Satan, too, refused a life of contemplation and submission. "His aim was no less than the throne of the universe."[66] Like a heavenly Faust, "rejoicing in his strength, walking colossal through heaven, gigantic in his conceptions, incessant in his working, ever scheming, ever imagining new enterprises, Satan was in his very nature the most active of God's archangels. He was ever doing some great thing, and ever thirsting for some greater thing to do."[67] Likewise, Pollok's Satan in *The Course of Time* is driven by burning thoughts to "act great deeds, though wicked" which brought not only punishment to the Faustian spirit but also the joy of striving, "the recompense which nature hath attached / To all activity, and aim, pursued / With perseverance, good or bad."

So compelling was Milton's portrayal of Satan, so perfectly did it coincide with the modern spirit of restless striving, and so strikingly did it anticipate the modern Faustian hero, that *Paradise Lost* became, like *Faust,* a history of an *Übermensch,* a history, as Masson described it, of Satan's experience "in the interval between his own fall and the fall of man,"[68] a poem not of plot but of "character and passion."[69] The reader went through Satan's history—just as he experienced the history of a hero of a modern novel—in order to understand him. "Satan is to be studied by following his progress."[70]

Satan's progress, of course, lay along the road of steady degeneration, and the Victorians were well aware of the fact. As John Wilson pointed out to the readers of *Blackwood's* "[Satan] is gradually brought down low, lower, lowest—by voluntary and imposed humiliation:—Self-incarnate in bestial slime—turned into a monstrous serpent on his belly prone, and hissing amongst hissing."[71] And although the Satan of *Paradise Regained* was the Satan of *Paradise Lost,* four thousand years of steady degeneration left him totally evil and shorn of all those qualities which at an earlier stage had evoked sympathy and admiration. Accordingly, Satan as he appeared in *Paradise Regained* was looked upon by the Victorians as a despicable creature who deserved no sympathy and merited little attention. George Gilfillan stated the typical view when he wrote that the Satan of the "Paradise Lost" had many elements of the heroic, and even when starting from his toad-shape, he recovers his grandeur instantly by his stature reaching the sky. But the Satan of the "Paradise Regained" is a mean, low, crawling worm—a little and limping fiend. He never looks the Saviour full in the face, but keeps nibbling at his heels. And although in this Milton has expressed the actual history of intellect and courage, when separated from virtue, happiness, and hope, and degraded into the servile vassals of an infernal will, yet it is not so pleasing for us to contemplate the completed as it is the begun ruin.[72]

In other words, the Satan of *Paradise Lost*—especially the Satan of the first two books—and not the Satan of *Paradise Regained,* was for the nineteenth century *the* Miltonic Satan. The sympathy and admiration of the Victorians could not be aroused by a being utterly devoid of a sublime and sympathetic character, but it was excited by what Masson called "the ruined archangel as he may be supposed to have existed at that epoch of the creation when he had hardly decided his own function; as yet warring with the Almighty, or, in pursuit of a gigantic scheme of revenge, travelling from star to star."[73]

In the popular religious epics of Pollok, Montgomery, and Heraud, the Miltonic Satan in all his magnificence and ruined splendor is described and portrayed time and again. Even when he appears to tempt the Messiah in the wilderness or when he is summoned to the Last Judgment, he is invariably the "archangel ruin'd" of *Paradise Lost.* All thoughts of degeneration are politely and tacitly put aside, and the being who was ambitious, proud, and revengeful but "yet not utterly devoid of pity and remorse"[74] appears upon the scene. "Descending from his secret place of storms," the Satan of Heraud's epic, *The Judgement of the Flood,* walks like a blasted titan across the epic landscape:

> His foot clanged resonant on the trembling ground,
> And his dilating presence royally
> Spread o'er the wild, his stature reached the sky.
> Gloomed o'er his brow the infernal diadem,
> Like a black crag projected o'er a cliff,

> White as the surge, the barrier of the main;
> And, like a blasted orb once over-bright,
> His eye, a ruin, burned; and on his cheek,
> Immortal Beauty hideously shone;
> A wreck as of a noble Ship long tost,
> Stanced, where it rived, amid the calmed sea,
> Sublime though desolate, and beautiful
> Though loveless.
>
> (p. 140)

In Robert Montgomery's *Satan,* a poem in which the hero soliloquizes in blank verse through six books, a Miltonic Satan greets us from the top of a great mountain swept by a fierce storm and wrapped in smoke and cloud (see p. 21) which recall to him that mighty day

> When proud rebellion shook the walls of Heaven,—
> Till, charioted by Thunder, forth He came,
> The lightning of the Lord, and blazed revenge,
> Hurling us downward to the deep of Hell,
> That madden'd wild as billows in the storm,
> When rushingly we met her roaring flames!
>
> (p. 22)

However, the reader soon realizes that a radical change has occurred. Satan has not further degenerated; rather he has regenerated into a very moral being who views the sins of the world with considerable distaste. One reviewer summed up the opinion of the press when he declared that Montgomery clothes Satan "in a new suit of clerical sable, and sets him to preach at the vices and follies of the world, as if he were a minister of the Gospel." Instead of aping Milton's Satan, "the noblest mythological personage ever created by poetry," the author portrays "a mere abstraction without shape or character or the pretense of individual feeling: it is," the indignant reviewer concluded, "utterly false to both the popular [i.e., medieval] and the Miltonic conceptions of the Devil."[75]

This, to be sure, was Montgomery's only deviation from the norm, for he really was very skillful at pleasing the public's taste for the fierce, untamed but nobly magnificent Satan of obvious Miltonic descent. In *The Messiah* when the temptation scenes occur, Montgomery deliberately inserted the sublime Satan of *Paradise Lost* into a sequence otherwise highly reminiscent of *Paradise Regained* (see p. 20). Instead of appearing as an old man, an Archimago, he comes in great splendor, bursting forth "from out the earth's unfathom'd deep,"

> Upon his brow the gloom of thunder sat,
> And in the darkness of his dreadful eye
> Lay the sheath'd lightnings of immortal ire!
> As King of dark eternity, he faced
> The Godhead; cent'ring in that one still glance
> The hate of Heav'n and the agony of Hell,
> Defiance and Despair!—and then, with voice
> Sepulchral, grand as when a tempest dies,
> Him thus address'd.
>
> (p. 106)

Finally when he appears again at the Last Judgment, he is the same Miltonic Satan as before:

> vast above the vastest there,
> In tow'ring majesty [Satan] confronts the sky,
> As though the fabric of the heavens would shrink
> From the dark light of his unfathom'd gaze,
> Behold him!—how magnificently dread!
> From the huge mountains into embers sunk,
> To the last billow of expiring sea,—
> O'er all, the terror of his ruin frowns
> Sublime, who battled with Omnipotence,
> And will be fearless in the fires of hell!
>
> (p. 246)

Heraud in *The Descent into Hell* illustrates the same principle. Four thousand years after his fall when Messiah triumphs over the grave, he is still not the completely degenerate Satan of *Paradise Regained*. When Messiah summons him, he arises "Majestic from the fiery lake." Despite his fallen state, "that quenchèd Star" is yet

> beauteous, though of glory shorn,
> Beautiful, but not lovely. . . . But, from Heaven
> Derived, his beauty springs, unalien since,
> Whence strength and vigour to his guilt are given,
> Greatness of Soul, and energy of will,
> Resolve majestic, column yet unriven,
> With valorous virtue, calm, sedate and still;
> Royal investments, worthy of man's foe,
> And God's Arch-angel though depraved to ill.[76]

There can be no doubt that the splendid figure of Satan—the nineteenth century's "archangel ruin'd"—was very appealing to the sympathetic imaginations of the time. And many felt that Milton, himself, was captivated by his own creation. "The reason Milton wrote in fetters," said Blake, "when he wrote of Angels and God, and at liberty when of Devils and Hell, is because he was a true Poet and of the Devil's party without knowing it."[77] A century later Walter Raleigh declared that Milton lavished "the greater part of his sympathy, on the splendid figure of Satan."[78] Walter Bagehot was of the opinion that

> though the *theme* of *Paradise Lost* obliged Milton to side with the monarchical element in the universe, his old habits are often too much for him; and his real sympathy—the impetus and energy of his nature—side with the rebellious element. . . . Milton's sympathy and his imagination slip back to the Puritan rebels whom he loved, and desert the courtly angels whom he could not love although he praised. There is no wonder that Milton's hell is better than his heaven, for he hated officials and he loved rebels, for he employs his genius below, and accumulates his pedantry above.[79]

Bagehot, here, of course, was following in the footsteps of Blake and Shelley who in their antipathy to Milton's God—the symbol of law, restraint, tradition, and tyranny—lavished all their sympathy on the Faustian nature of Satan who "perseveres in a purpose which he has conceived to be excellent, in spite of adversity and torture."[80] Satan, in their eyes, was redeemed by his life of action and saved by attempting to fulfill his own potentialities at all costs. On the other hand, Milton's God, unlike the "modern" God of *Faust,* is an evil tyrant because he

Satan arousing the Fallen Angels

Adam and Eve driven out of Paradise

The Angels guarding Paradise at night

imposes restrictions, expects a life of contemplation and stasis, and, therefore, condones the greatest sin to a Faustian mind, contentment. That is why Shelley could say that Milton's Devil, as a moral being, is far superior to his God, and why Bagehot could believe that "in *Paradise Lost* it is always clear that the devils are the weaker, but it is never clear that the angels are the better."[81] According to the views of these men, Milton was a Faustian modern spirit (just as Schiller had said he was) who revealed his true self in the character of Satan.[82]

This problem of sympathizing with Satan, the source of all woes, was not a serious one before the nineteenth century simply because Milton's readers had earlier been able to see Satan in a proper perspective, that is, as one of several characters in a Christian epic the plot of which—the most important element— centered on the fall and redemption of mankind. The seventeenth- and eighteenth-century reader reacted to Milton's Satan with horror and revulsion. But by the close of the eighteenth century, that strangely modern feeling of aspiration, that insatiable desire to know all things and do all things and scorn all restraint, was beginning to permeate the culture of the Western World. Men once restrained and limited by tradition suddenly, after the Enlightenment, felt free and unlimited. Many now divested of the knowledge of certain truth were impelled to search for it till they died or satisfied themselves that they had found it again through experience; and men and nations, elated by the feeling of infinite power which machines and science instilled in them, labored like titans under the illusion that their possibilities were limitless.

Accordingly, a being whose thoughts wandered through eternity and whose unconquerable will refused to submit or yield to a Supreme Being who of necessity had to represent restraint and conceal ultimate knowledge, became immediately attractive and extremely sympathetic. The nineteenth century, therefore, looked on Satan as a heroic figure whose torment, struggle and aspiration chimed in tune with their own feelings. Intellectually some might condemn him for "having pursued action too much," and for having "spurned worship and contemplation,"[83] but emotionally they sympathized and agreed with Faust's God that men make mistakes as long as they strive, but strive they must or be damned forever.

This sympathetic identification with the Miltonic Satan was so pervasive and keen, that many clergymen and laymen alike became alarmed and found it a danger to the moral well-being of the nation. In his lecture "On the Characteristics of True Poetry" which he gave before the Roman Catholic Instruction Society in 1849, John Henry Newman, turning to Milton's *Paradise Lost,* agreed with Dryden that Satan was not only the principal character in the epic but also the hero. Moreover, Satan "is assigned the most prominent place, and he is also made the most poetical person in the poem."

> The *poetry* of Milton's mind has made the evil spirits beautiful, and this is wrong, and even dangerous, as wherever evil is poetised, and therefore made beautiful, it is a dangerous departure from truth, not only theological and religious, but even moral. This principle is exemplified in Byron's "Cain," where the character of the first murderer is made a beautiful one; and when Byron was censured for this, he defended himself by the example of Milton, who had made Satan poetical.

Then Newman read Milton's description of the colloquy between Satan and Beelzebub and added: "So long as pride is made beautiful by the poet, so also will there be poetry evil in its tendencies, in which the worst vices will be poetised and rendered attractive."[84]

Similarly, the Reverend F. A. Cox, in an article in *The Journal of Sacred Literature* declared "that the moral influence of the portraiture of Satan has had a detrimental effect on some minds, especially on those of a high poetic temperament, such as Byron and Shelley. . . . We might not have had 'Cain' if we had never had *Paradise Lost."* Without hesitation the minister stated that the reader "is lost in the hero [Satan], and there is a tendency to take part with the proud and the daring adventurer figuring as a demigod at the head of embattled hosts. His reverses are beheld with feelings of commiseration, and his exploits with approval and triumph." Milton's superb portrayal of the fallen but yet magnificent archangel has probably encouraged "the too prevalent admiration of pomp, ambition, and conquest."[85]

John Ruskin, for different reasons, was also dissatisfied with Satan. In a statement which points out the precise difference between the medieval devil and the Miltonic Satan, Ruskin remarked that "Milton makes his fiends too noble, and misses the foulness, inconstancy, and fury of wickedness. His Satan possesses some virtues, not the less virtues for being applied to evil purpose. Courage, resolution, patience, deliberation in counsel, this latter being eminently a wise and holy character, as opposed to the 'Insania' of excessive sin: and all this, if not shallow and false, is a smoothed and artificial, conception."[86] Of course, it was the noble possessor of "some virtues" that appealed to the nineteenth-century readers of Montgomery and Heraud and not the grotesque inhuman devils that seemed more true and real to Ruskin.

But as the nineteenth century waned, the attractions of the Miltonic Satan were gradually disregarded as Victorian bourgeois complacency destroyed the taste for the heroic, and the high adventure and cosmic drama of the epic gave way to the more commonplace, everyday incidents of the novel. This large general shift away from the heroic, discussed at length in Mario Praz's *The Hero in Eclipse,* together with the decline in interest in the Bible and a Satanic being, bereft Satan of his age-old appeal. Throughout the century there was a tendency to lose faith in a grotesque, all-evil being, and the Victorians seconded Hazlitt's praise of a Satan without horns and tail. Later, however, even the Miltonic Satan, the Satan with the mental and physical attributes of a human being, faded away, dissolved by the reader's inability to comprehend anything metaphysical, anything, that is, beyond the scientific grasp of reality.

Speaking about "Hell" and the "Devil," Masson as early as 1844 said that "the spirit of these words has become obsolete, chased away by the spirit of exposition. . . . The going out of the belief in Satanic agency (for even those who retain it in profession allow it no force in practice), M. Comte would attribute to the progress of the spirit of that philosophy of which he is the apostle [i.e., the scientific spirit of Positivism]." But Masson accounted for it "by the going out, in the progress of civilization, of those sensations which seem naturally fitted to nourish the belief in supernatural beings. The tendency of civilization has been to diminish our opportunities of feeling terror, of feeling strongly at all. The horrific plays a much less important part in human experience than it once did."[87]

Walter Raleigh expressed the sentiments of the late nineteenth century when he declared: "Satan himself is not what he used to be; he is doubly fallen, in the esteem of his victims as well as of his Maker, and indeed

> Comes to the place where he before had sat
> Among the prime in splendour, now deposed,
> Ejected, emptied, gazed, unpitied, shunned,
> A spectacle of ruin."[88]

V   Although the ridicule of the critics in time lessened its popularity, the religious epic imitative of Milton continued to be written and read. In 1838 William Herbert's *Attila, or the Triumph of Christianity,*[89] an epic in twelve books, appeared; and in 1839 Robert Montgomery published *A Dream of Worlds.* In this same year, Philip James Bailey published *Festus,* and since the earlier successes of Montgomery, no poem had caused such a rage among the Victorian readers as this one.

Bailey began *Festus* as an imitation of Goethe's *Faust,* but as the long poem continues to be revised, it becomes more and more Miltonic in style and diction.[90] Its Lucifer also is highly reminiscent of Milton's Satan, especially in the later episodes of the revisions. The epic is interesting in that it illustrates how easily elements from *Faust* and certain aspects of *Paradise Lost* mingled together rather naturally in the Victorian mind. And although *Festus* is thought of by many as one of the chief glories of the Spasmodic school of poetry, it has elements in common with the Miltonic religious poetry—cosmic setting, supernatural characters, extravagant rhetoric, style, and diction. In fact, some if not all of these elements are found in most of the poetry of the Spasmodics, and the apparent similarities between the two groups suggest that the apocalyptic poetry was an early manifestation or stage of what later was termed by Charles Kingsley that "spasmodic, vague, extravagant, effeminate school of poetry."[91]

Naturally enough, the poetry of the Spasmodics as a whole is not relevant here simply because it is not directly imitative of Milton and because it often deals more directly with contemporary social problems than does the religious epic discussed here, although Montgomery's *Satan* with its survey of the contemporary scene might be cited as an exception.

But Bailey wrote several Miltonic religious epics in the 1850's of which *A Spiritual Legend,* later incorporated into *Festus,* is an interesting example. It displays all the usual characteristics of the religious epic and focuses on the angels who, desirous of tidying up chaos—that "dark material mass, / Malignant, uncreate, inert, self-lived," which lay below—obtain God's consent to create the world and place a new creature there. Their "work orbific" begins, and

> Soon, distinct,
> Ocean and continent, sea, desert, plain
> Mineral and vegetive, concrete, complete,
> By separate hand, each Power a separate type
> Framing, to grace his will, or prove his force,
> Of stone, earth, tree, plant, shrub, grass, herb, or flower,
> Mountain, or isle, or river, lake, or well.[92]

Each mountain, "bulk by bulk, / And chain by chain," is fabricated:

> Hekla and Mouna Roa and Auvergne;
> Tuxtla; and Tongarari, southwards isled;
> By savages beset, who deem, when dead,

> Their chieftain's eyes translated into stars;
> Andes and Himalaya's heavenly heights;
> Dhawalaghiri's pinnacle supreme,
> And Chuquibamba's cone of roseate snow.
>
>   (p. 73)

But, in time, the angels are corrupted through pride and

> seeking at first,
> Their own names, to the tribes each emperor'd,
> To magnify, and so become their gods;
> In lieu of teaching man the one supreme
> To worship, God; whom all alike were bound
> To honor and adore. Through this they fell;
> (No longer kind to man, whate'er to God;)
> The angels fell, and drew down earth with them.
>
>   (p. 113)

The pagan gods are now described at length including Hephaistos, "the same / Whom later Greeks named architect of heaven," and the "Head of the angel race, prime demiurge," who plays the part of Satan. Man, at last, however, is redeemed by the Messiah and the epic ends with the triumph of good.

Such religious epics appear fairly steadily from the 1820's to the mid-Victorian era and show just how long a general tradition of Miltonic imitation persisted. Referring to the Miltonic elements in Bailey's poetry, R. D. Havens says that "Bailey's *Angel World, The Mystic,* and *A Spiritual Legend* are, in diction and in the extensive use of strange proper nouns, astonishingly Miltonic for poems published as late as 1850 and 1855."[93]

Often almost completely ignored as poetry, these epics are of obvious value when one is attempting to gauge the temper of the times or the attitude of a generation toward Milton. Many early Victorians read Milton's poetry and that of his imitators because it displayed elements which appealed to their "religious imagination." When this religious imagination began to lose its vitality, the religious poets lost their public and so did the apocalyptic painters. Balston remarks that by the time of John Martin's death in 1854 "the flight from imagination was beginning, especially religious imagination. By 1880 a Biblical illustration in a drawing-room was as compromising as a Bible. Martin's works moved upstairs to bedrooms and to attics."[94] Of course, Milton's poetry, unlike the poetry of his imitators, survived the decline in the religious imagination because, like all great poetry, it is something like a kaleidoscope which exhibits aspects forever various and new. When the grandeur, sublimity, and heroic character of Satan failed to attract attention, and the religious aspects of *Paradise Lost* became passé, Milton's consummate artistry, as we shall see, continued to attract admirers.

V ᵍ Milton the Puritan: Pro and Con

*I am not sure that the greatest man of his
age, if ever that solitary superlative existed,
could escape these unfavorable reflections of
himself in various small mirrors; and even Milton,
looking for his portrait in a spoon, must submit
to have the facial angle of a bumpkin.*
—GEORGE ELIOT, *Middlemarch*

I

ALTHOUGH THERE has been some question in the twentieth century as to what extent Milton was a Puritan,[1] there was surely no uncertainty in the minds of the Victorians. "No Puritan, not Cromwell himself," said Peter Bayne, "was more Puritan than Milton."[2] And in the opinion of John Ruskin, "Not the Bible, but Milton's poem, on the one side, and Bunyan's prose, on the other, formed the English Puritan mind."[3] Consequently, Puritanism is the key, in many respects, to the Victorian attitude toward Milton's character, politics, and religion.

Generally speaking, there were three Victorian approaches to Milton the Puritan. Those who sympathized with a strong monarchy and were members of the Tory aristocracy, the High Church party, and the Roman Catholic communion, often liked to picture Milton the dissenter and republican as a sour, unsympathetic, stern and narrow Puritan, and they usually employed the word "puritan" as a term of disapproval and ridicule. Their essential attitude was expressed by John Wilson who said that Milton was a "great poet; but a bad divine, and a miserable politician."[4] On the other hand, the dissenters, Evangelicals,

Whigs, and radicals also thought of Milton as a Puritan, but in their context the word "puritan" was a term of approbation, and was used to describe a great religious poet, a Puritan saint who was a serious-minded, solemn, and lofty prophet, and a vigorous, dynamic advocate of religious and political freedom. Then there were those who had a less biased, more historically correct concept of Puritanism who believed that Milton was basically a Puritan but a great deal more besides, with none of the harsher, more extreme qualities often incorrectly attributed to the sect.

It is important to remember that until the nineteenth century Milton criticism was dominated by critics sympathetic to the Tory cause and the ideals of the Anglican church. Furthermore, the eighteenth-century biographers, at least the most influential ones, were also Tory-Anglicans.[5] Consequently, eighteenth-century biographies of Milton (with the exception of Addison's critical commentaries) are usually biased and unbalanced and often exhibit a marked distaste for Milton's character and eschew his political and religious ideals. This type of biography and criticism written from the Tory-Anglican point of view reigned supreme in the eighteenth century and, after a marked decline, continued throughout the nineteenth and has persisted with all its distinguishing features even to the present time.

From the beginning even its most enlightened practitioners have continued to see the Puritans, including Milton, in a very special light: as men, they were, as Matthew Arnold so perfectly expressed it, "unamiable." Milton, according to Dr. Johnson, was a "severe and arbitrary" man, who had "something like a Turkish contempt of females" and who was in politics "an acrimonious and surly republican."[6] "As a man," remarked T. S. Eliot, Milton "is antipathetic. Either from the moralist's point of view, or from the psychologist's point of view, or from that of the political philosopher, or judging by the ordinary standards of likeableness in human beings, Milton is unsatisfactory."[7] This tone and attitude expressed in the writings of Johnson, Arnold, and Eliot are typical of a point

of view which goes back to the sixteenth century when Royalists
and advocates of High Church Anglicanism first employed the
word "puritan" as a term of ridicule to be applied to divines
such as Thomas Cartwright who refused to go along with the
halfway reform condoned by Elizabeth and who were determined to see, sooner or later, a complete reform of the Established Church.[8]

Long before the Restoration, a deliberate campaign had
begun to label the reformers with a term of contempt and derision. The Puritans, of course, were early aware of these tactics
to misrepresent their character and aims. For instance, it is
interesting to read a work such as Mrs. Hutchinson's *Memoirs
of the Life of Colonel Hutchinson,* in which she at times sought
to expose these attempts to ridicule the Puritans out of existence by using the word to connote the most distasteful, extravagant, and exaggerated aspects of Puritanism. During the time
of James I, she wrote, ministers who preached against the vice
and lewdness of the court and nobles were "hated, disgraced,
and reviled, and in scorn had the name of Puritan fixed upon
them. . . . In short," continued the writer,

> all that crossed the views of the needy courtiers, the proud en-
> croaching priests, the thievish projectors, the lewd nobility and
> gentry—whoever was zealous for God's glory or worship, could
> not endure blasphemous oaths, ribald conversation, profane scoffs,
> Sabbath-breaking, derision of the word of God, and the like—
> whoever could endure a sermon, modest habit or conversation, or
> anything good,—all these were Puritans; and if Puritans, then
> enemies to the king and his government, seditious, factious hypo-
> crites, ambitious disturbers of the public peace, and finally, the
> pest of the kingdom.[9]

After the Restoration, as David Masson pointed out, the
previous tactics were revived, and there was a "literary crusade
against the Puritans, as canting, sour-visaged, mirth-forbidding,
art-abhorring religionists, which came to its height at the time
when Butler wrote his Hudibras, and Wycherley his plays."[10]
As a result, by 1830 it was a tradition for those who disliked

the temperament and ideals of dissenters to resort to the practice of calling them Puritans, which was the same as calling them harsh, hypocritical, dour, and unamiable killjoys. It is no wonder that the word which was conceived in derision and fostered in an atmosphere of hate and disgust has had and perhaps always will have its unfortunate and unpleasant connotations.

Certainly, the Victorians, like most people, were misled into believing that the Puritans were the severe and horribly warped creatures of the Tory imagination. One Victorian was witness to this fact when he asserted that his contemporaries viewed the Puritans of the seventeenth century "through the partial sketches of Clarendon, through the distorting glass of *Hudibras,* or through their own acts and writings after their passions had been roused by oppression, or inflamed by victory. We ascribe," he continued, "to them in the mass, the wild dreams of the Fifth Monarchy men, the root-and-branch work of the Independents, and the hallucinations of the younger Vane and George Fox, the bitterness of Prynne, and the peevishness of Sir Simon D'Ewes. All their elders, viewed through this medium, are as Zeal-in-the-land-Busy; all their soldiers as Corporal Have-the-grace-Holdfast; all their preachers as Hugh Peters."[11]

But during the early years of the nineteenth century, a pronounced reaction to the Tory biographical and critical approach to Milton occurred, signaled, in part, by Macaulay's famous essay of 1825; and by the third decade, a new and radically different approach to Milton biography was being employed by several writers sympathetic to the ideals of the dissenters, Whigs, liberals, and radicals. The new biographies written by Joseph Ivimey, William Carpenter, Cyrus Edmonds, Edwin Paxton Hood, and others were dedicated to the propagation of Milton's political and religious views and activities, and, of necessity, to the exposition of the prose rather than the poetry. This important new direction in Milton biography was accompanied by clear and concise objections to the previous

biographical writings, and succinct statements as to the aims
and purposes of the new.

In general, the objections to Tory biography were two. First,
the biographies by Dr. Johnson and his contemporaries, members of the English church and Tory party, were biased and
unsympathetic to Milton, the republican and dissenter; and, in
turn, this bias resulted in unbalanced and ill-proportioned
biographies which over-emphasized the poetry and slighted the
prose. That is, the eighteenth-century biographer usually found
it more congenial to talk about Milton's poetry than to discuss
his prose, and Milton the poet was more appealing than Milton
the man. Second, the biographies were printed in large, elaborate editions which were too expensive for the poorer classes
to buy.

Cyrus Edmonds in the preface to *John Milton: a biography
especially designed to exhibit the ecclesiastical principles of
that illustrious man,* stated the first and major objection most
clearly. The Puritans, he believed, had in the past been portrayed by men incapable of understanding their character and
committed by political considerations to misrepresent their
conduct. The most potent cause of neglect of Milton's political
and religious ideas and his prose was, he declared, that he was
a Puritan and the Puritans unfortunately had been depicted by
their opponents. "His most eminent biographers, as members
of the Church of England, have had no sympathy with their
illustrious subject in the grandest phase which his character
and his writings present."[12]

Similarly, Robert Fletcher, the editor of *The Prose Works
of John Milton* (1835), a new and popular edition, in "An
Introductory Review," informed his readers that "Milton's
moral and intellectual character has, for a long while, been
tacitly placed under the guardianship of his most bitter antag-
onists. It unfortunately happens that the most popular of his
biographers is his most malignant traducer."[13] In this and other
references to Dr. Johnson, Fletcher was typical of the new
biographers who found Dr. Johnson's *Life of Milton* extremely

offensive because it was the most widely read and influential Milton biography of the day, and had come to be the epitome of the Tory approach to Milton's life. In fact, the influence of Johnson's *Life* was so great and—to Fletcher—so baneful, that he in exasperation exclaimed, "Who that (and what numbers!) have formed their estimate of his [Milton's] Prose Works from that [Dr. Johnson's] account of them would have any idea of their real merits?"[14]

Joseph Ivimey, a Baptist preacher, and author of *John Milton: His Life and Times, Religious and Political Opinions* (1833), assured his readers that Dr. Johnson's "ultra-toryism and bigotry" blinded him to Milton's true character and opinion. Since Johnson's "obnoxious work" formed a part of "that standard publication," *The Lives of the British Poets,* Ivimey found it necessary to write his "Animadversions on Dr. Johnson's Life of Milton" in order to counteract the false, biased, and unbalanced views of Milton which it propagated.[15] Indeed, the reaction to Johnson was so hostile and widespread during the early Victorian period, that a reviewer in *Hogg's Instructor* spoke for a large and representative audience when he declared that when reading Johnson's life and critical estimate of Milton, "we are moved alternately to smiles and sneers, and feel at one moment inclined to pity, and at another to pillory the strong-minded, but pedantic and prejudiced old Jacobite."[16] And it was Walter Raleigh's opinion that Dr. Johnson was the best of all Milton's critics, but he left us "the worst account of his political opinions."[17]

That Milton's poetry had been emphasized to the detriment of his prose was touched upon by Ivimey when he indicated that "the former biographers of Milton have exhibited him principally in his character as a *poet,* but have obscured his features as a *patriot,* a *protestant,* and *non-conformist.*"[18] Indeed, the Tory biographers made it a policy to repress "what we deem," said William Carpenter in *The Life and Times of John Milton* (1836), "to be the more noble qualities of his [Milton's] intellect and his heart, and in keeping out of sight the more practically valuable and honourable portion of his literary labour."[19] In more picturesque terms, Fletcher wrote that in Milton biography, "the poet has long eclipsed the man;—he has been imprisoned even in the temple of the muses; and the very splendour of the bard seems to be our title to pass 'an act of oblivion' on the share he bore in the events and discussions of the momentous times in which he lived."[20] And again Fletcher was expressing the view of Ivimey, Carpenter, and others when he stated why the poetry was attractive and congenial to the Tory biographers whereas the prose was not. "Prelates, and tithes and kings, were not the burthen of his [Milton's] song, and therefore the poetry can be praised even by those whose souls were wrapped up in these things. While he soared away 'in the high reason of his fancies,' and meddled not with the practical affairs of life, his enemies can be complimentary, and undertake to bow him into immortality." But, on the other hand, his earlier biographers "would fain suppress all other monuments of this Englishman:—it remains for us to appreciate them. Let us never think of John Milton as a poet merely, however in that capacity he may have adorned our language, and benefitted, by ennobling, his species. He was a citizen also, with whom patriotism was as heroical a passion, prompting him to do his country service, as was that 'inward prompting' of poesy, by which he did his country honour."[21]

Finally, there were many objections to lengthy, elaborate, and expensive biographies which were out of the reach of most people. In speaking of Symmons' *Life of Milton,* William Carpenter noted that it was too voluminous "for general circulation and too discursive and critical for popular reading."[22] Joseph Ivimey announced that another reason which prompted him to attempt a new biography was "that the Lives of Milton have usually been so large and expensive, that they have been placed out of the reach of the generality of readers." Ivimey hoped that his "small volume, comprising everything of importance respecting this noble-minded and gigantic man, will not be unacceptable nor unprofitable to the bulk of his countrymen."[23]

Likewise, Edwin Paxton Hood, in dedicating his *John Milton: the Patriot and Poet* to the young men of England, declared that "Love and reverence" might have expanded his volume "to a heavier bulk and price; but in this case, the main intention of the compiler would have been defeated, which was to furnish as good a copy of the venerable portrait as he could, for the sum of one shilling and sixpence."[24] This attitude toward Milton biography is an early indication of the desire more clearly manifest later—especially in the criticisms of Masson's *Life of Milton*—to pare down the biographies to a concise, simple statement of pertinent facts and to publish them in inexpensive editions so that the poorer classes could avail themselves of the information. Since the new biographers thought of Milton and his prose as being of great *practical* importance to the people, their desire for this type of biography was especially great at the time.

Of course, among the aims and purposes of the new biographies was the remedying of those things objected to—bias, unbalanced accounts, and expensive editions, and although the desire to write more balanced accounts of Milton's life—"to write the history of a man who united in himself the two high and honourable characters of Patriot and Poet"[25]—was strong, the principal aim was to see the religious and political sentiments of Milton "justly appreciated." As Edmonds declared, his purpose in writing a new biography was "to present Milton afresh to the public as the champion of political, and especially of religious liberty."[26] To do this, naturally, meant that the prose would come to the fore and the poetry would be allotted a less important part. Ivimey wanted to give "an accurate and full-length portrait" of Milton, "the most eminent of our countrymen"; but "for the purpose of accomplishing this design," he declared, it was necessary to make "considerable extracts from the *prose* writings of Milton, by which, in a good degree, he appears as his own biographer."[27]

This revival of interest in Milton's prose writings is the most important consequence of the new biography; for, without doubt, it did bring Milton's prose works back from almost total oblivion. "John Milton's [prose] works have been long buried," said Robert Fletcher, "but they are not consumed;—long neglected, but they are not injured."[28] As a result, the biographies of Ivimey, Edmonds, Hood, and Carpenter dealt almost entirely with the prose. By generous extracts, résumés and long descriptive analyses of *all* the prose works, the new biographers, along with new editions of the prose such as John Mitford's and the influential Bohn Library edition, made it possible for the Victorians to know the religious and political views of Milton in detail.

To be sure, Macaulay in his Milton essay of 1825 had spoken well in passing of Milton's prose works, and the young Thomas Carlyle, contemplating a lengthy study of Milton, had read them through with enthusiasm;[29] but until the 1830's there was no concerted effort such as these biographers made to rescue all of Milton's prose writings from the curse of disuse. "It is astonishing," wrote Fletcher in 1833, "that these books [the prose works] should not in our time have been appreciated by the people, and it is greatly to be regretted, not merely for the sake of their author, but for the general interests of truth, and the cultivation of learning, eloquence, and taste amongst us, that they should be so little read."[30] And although Fletcher was willing to admit that "the summit of fame" is occupied by Milton, the poet, "the base of the vast elevation," he continued, "may justly be said to rest on these Prose Works; and we invite his admirers to descend from the former, and survey the region that lies round about the latter,—a less explored, but not less magnificent, domain."[31]

In the introduction to his important and inexpensive edition of Milton's prose works, Fletcher made the point that Milton's character could best be known through a study of his prose which is interspersed with ample autobiographical passages. Milton the poet is well-known, he wrote, but Milton the man is best known through his prose which has been neglected. Let his prose be read, and Milton will disperse the lies and errors

about himself propagated by the Tories. Then Fletcher prophesied a new era of truth in the domain of Milton studies when
he declared that Dr. Johnson's

> misrepresentations and calumnies, and that heartless faction of
> which he was certainly an eminent representative, have had their
> day: and inconceivably injurious though they have been to the
> honour of John Milton, sure we are that the time is fast approach-
> ing, yea now is, when the man as well as the poet shall be redeemed
> from obloquy. . . . Let him but be heard. The charges against him
> are in all hands; here, in this one volume, is to be found their
> triumphant, but neglected, refutation.[32]

Joseph Ivimey, of like mind, also felt that an era of
better feeing toward the prose was opening. "The prejudice,"
he wrote, "which has existed against Milton's prose works, on
account of his republican and dissenting principles, fully accounts for their having been so little known; but it is hoped
that such feelings are rapidly subsiding, if they are not yet become quite extinct."[33] To be sure, the prejudice had not dis-
appeared, but Milton's prose was to become rather popular,
especially with the Chartists who sought to establish a government in England similar to the ideal republic outlined by Milton
in his prose works. The enthusiasm for Milton's writings can
clearly be seen in the epigraphs and extracts from "The Tenure
of Kings and Magistrates," "Eikonoklastes," "The Ready and
Easy Way to Establish a Free Commonwealth," and others
which appeared constantly in such publications as *The Chartist
Circular*.[34] Believing that Milton was a thorough-going democrat, the Chartist and other radical groups found Milton's defense of freedom and republican government extremely congenial and beneficial to their cause.[35]

Although the biographers and editors of Milton's prose that
I have mentioned were perhaps just as biased in their own way
as the eighteenth-century biographers were in theirs, the work
of these men had far-reaching and salutary effects on Milton
studies during the Victorian period. For instance, Milton's
prose was reconsidered favorably by later critics of worth who

sought to understand and defend them, and Milton biographies throughout the remainder of the century tended to be short and concise, with the one major exception of Masson's *Life of Milton,* which was severely criticized for its length and compass. The three other most notable and valuable lives published during the second half of the century—Keightley's, Pattison's, and Raleigh's—were short, concise, well-balanced biographies which sought to portray the whole man in all his important aspects. It is interesting, too, to notice how careful these men were to discuss fully and fairly Milton's prose works. In this respect, Keightley's—the first to be published—is the most noteworthy.

Generally speaking, then the new biographers' emphasis on Milton's prose helped bring about three important changes in the status of Milton's works. First, new editions of the prose such as Fletcher's were published as well as a number of extremely inexpensive copies of single works. For instance, bound in with William Carpenter's *Life of Milton* were "cheap reprints" of *Areopagitica* and "Considerations touching the likeliest means to remove Hirelings out of the Church," which also sold separately for six pence apiece. Second, the later biographies of Milton were less biased and unbalanced, and third, the attitude toward Milton's prose became much more favorable as the century progressed. Certainly Masson was not alone among his contemporaries in believing that Milton was one of the great prose writers in English: "Suffice it to say, that both as regards style and matter, his [Milton's] prose-writings are among the most magnificent and powerful in the English language, and that if ever there was a time when they should be read and studied, that time is the present."[36] And Robert Wallace went so far as to state that as a prose writer, Milton "excelled all his contemporaries, rich as England then was in writers of that class."[37] Later, Edward Dowden remarked that behind all that is occasional in the prose works, "what gives these writings an enduring value—a series of ideals, more lofty, complete, and in a high sense reasonable, than can readily be found elsewhere among his contemporaries, ideals for the domestic and the corporate life of England, which form a lasting contribution to the higher thought of our country."[38]

These comments emphatically demonstrate the noteworthy shift in sentiment which occurred in the first half of the nineteenth century. Instead of finding every conceivable reason to slander Milton's prose writings and leave them unread, from Fletcher and Carpenter onward, numerous attempts were made to defend them and to represent them in the best light. For example, Ivimey early noticed that Milton's prose writings were not as scurrilous as the Tories made them out to be. "From his memoirs having been written by Churchmen who must have necessarily disapproved of his opinions," he wrote, "it is not wonderful that he should have been charged with employing 'coarse and intemperate,' 'rude and insulting language.' "[39] However, Walter Raleigh made a better defense when he pointed out that "there is nothing wherein our age more differs from his [Milton's] than in the accepted rules governing controversy." As a result, he continued, Milton's prose has been viciously attacked by his opponents who have sought to heap upon it universal reproach. But "the most scurrilous of Milton's pamphlets," he declared, "were written in Latin, a language which has always enjoyed an excellent liberty in the matter of personal abuse; while even his English pamphlets, wherein at times he shows almost as pretty a talent in reviling, were written for an audience inured to the habitual amenities of Latin controversy." Raleigh, too, was quick to point out that Sir Thomas More "was famous for his knack of calling bad names in good Latin, yet his posterity rise up and call him blessed. Milton, like More, observed the rules of the game, which allowed practices condemned in the modern literary prize-ring."[40]

II   With the appearance on the literary scene of a new kind of Milton biography that sought to popularize the poet's religious and political ideals by reviving interest in the prose, Milton at last was represented by a sizeable group of writers sympathetic to his republican and Puritan principles who made a concerted effort to destroy the Tory image of Milton, or at least to present the people with what they believed to be an even more important facet of his character and thought. Although Carpenter, Edmonds, and writers of like mind were successful in giving the prose a new lease on life and in aiding the public and later biographers to see Milton in a more well-rounded way, the Tory biographers were not destroyed and continued to portray Milton as a great poet unfortunately tainted by Puritanism.[41]

In fact, throughout the Victorian period there were men who actually hated Milton, and others less rabid who continued the old royalist–High Church tactic of blackening his name by associating it with the harsh, hateful Puritan killjoy. Aided by the Oxford Movement and later schools interested in medievalism, the age-old campaign to castigate the Puritan type and its ideals continued at times with much verve. But it must be remembered that the dominant view of Milton as the stern, austere Puritan, which persisted throughout the century, was the result not only of an outright attempt to heap scorn on Milton the Puritan by emphasizing and exaggerating the more extreme and unpopular aspects of Puritanism, but also the result of the honest belief on the part of many that Milton either *unfortunately* had the temper and characteristics of the stern Puritan, or *fortunately* had the qualities of austerity and aloofness proper and fitting for a great religious poet and seer.

Certainly the most extreme descriptions of the stern Puritan Milton came, for the most part, from the pens of High Churchmen to whom the name of Milton was anathema. For instance, Hurrell Froude, an early leader of the Oxford Movement and close friend of Pusey, Keble, and Newman, reacted violently to Milton. The upbringing and education of Froude, the son of a High Church clergyman, was probably strongly influenced by the reaction of some Anglicans to the rising tide of liberalism and the resurgent strength of the dissenter groups during the 1820's. His more famous brother, James Anthony, remembered the Anglican reaction to the radicals and Puritans which led to the Oxford Movement, and once reported that "history was reconstructed for us. I had learnt, like other Protestant children, that the pope was Antichrist, and that Gregory VII had been a special revelation of that being. I was now taught that Gregory VII was a saint. I had been told to honour the Reformers. The Reformation became the great schism, Cranmer a traitor, and Latimer a vulgar ranter. Milton was a name of horror, and Charles I was canonized and spoken of as the holy and blessed Martyr St. Charles."[42]

James, of course, felt that the whole Oxford Movement was a tempest in a teapot, but his brother, Hurrell, took it very seriously, and was received into the Church of Rome before his early death. Truly Milton was a "name of horror" to him, and he made no secret of it. "I am glad I know something of the Puritans," he wrote in a letter to John Keble, "as it gives me a better right to hate Milton, and accounts for many of the things which most disgusted me in his not-in-my-sense-of-the-word poetry. Also, I adore King Charles and Bishop Laud."[43] Another High Churchman who disliked Milton and often referred to him as "that Puritan thief," the Reverend Robert Stephen Hawker, was so unsympathetic toward the man that he allowed his dislike to extend even to the metre of Milton's poetry. In a letter to F. G. Lee, the author of a prize poem in blank verse, Hawker asked,

> But why in rhymeless verses? You, too, who can rule the sound so well. It may be that I rather eschew the metre from horror at the false fame of that double-dyed thief of other men's brains—John Milton, the Puritan—one half of whose lauded passages are, *from my own knowledge,* felonies committed in the course of his reading on the property of others; and who was never so rightly appreciated, as by the publisher, who gave him fifteen pounds for the copywright of his huge larcenies, and was a natural loser by the bargain.[44]

However, the more usual description of Milton and the Puritans which Milton's detractors employed was imitated very well by Macaulay when he put in the mouth of Abraham Cowley the typical royalist view. "After Charles I was beheaded," declared Cowley in an imaginary conversation with Milton, "religion changed her nature. She was no longer the parent of arts and letters, of wholesome knowledge, of innocent pleasures, of blessed household smiles. In their place came sour faces, whining voices, the chattering of fools, the yells of madmen. Then men fasted from meat and drink, who fasted not from bribes and blood. Then men frowned at stage-plays, who smiled at massacres."[45] Furthermore, this view was carried over into fiction and is clearly reflected in a popular novel of 1881, Joseph Henry Shorthouse's *John Inglesant*. Shorthouse, who gave up his simple Quakerism for membership in the High Church, portrayed in this novel the life of a young man who acted as a liaison between the Catholics and Anglicans during the Civil War. Milton, Cromwell, and Henry More appear as characters in this novel, which paints a very attractive picture of the Papists and Laudians and describes the Puritans in typical royalist fashion. Inglesant's rival for the hand of Mary, the belle of the book, is Mr. Thorne, a stern, ill-humored, boorish Puritan who lectures and reproves his companions and displays all the gestures which Puritans were supposed automatically to make. For example, when Thorne takes his leave of Mary, he rises and presses her hand lightly, then raises his eyes to heaven "as the Puritans were ridiculed for doing."[46] Shorthouse, too, pictured the Puritans as men who condemned themselves and others during the Commonwealth to years "of shadowy gloom and of a morose antipathy to all delight." However, upon the return of Charles II, Shorthouse told his readers, there was "a restoration of a cheerful gaiety, and adorning of men's lives, when painting and poetry, and, beyond all, music, . . . smoothed the rough ways and softened the hard manners of men."[47]

No doubt, it was this idea of the Puritans as enemies of art and joy that caused William Morris, a contemporary of Shorthouse, to recoil from any contact with Milton. Morris evidently never found Milton's poetry congenial because of his antipathy to the poet's Puritanism. Once he remarked that "the union in his [Milton's] works of cold classicalism with Puritanism (the two things which I hate most in the world) repels me so that I *cannot* read him."[48]

However, it was not always the High Churchman who intemperately abused the Puritan poet. Samuel Roberts, a Sheffield silversmith who despised any but the lowest and plainest of worship services, evidently thought Milton was too close to the Anglicans. As a result, he devoted a whole volume, *Milton Unmasked,* to a tirade against the abominable Milton and his blasphemous *Paradise Lost.* Early in youth Roberts became "disgusted" with the character of Milton, and later came to consider *Paradise Lost* "one of the most unholy, uninteresting, and mischievous books that was ever published."[49] The Divine Personages in the epic, he declared, "are daringly introduced together with the devil and his angels, as leading heroes; and are all made to speak and to act just in the way that the author of the impious work has chosen that they should do, for the purpose of displaying his supposed superlative talent."[50] With fashionable Christians who must have "sumptuous temples, painted windows, graceful habiliments, enchanting music, hired singing men and singing women," *Paradise Lost* with its sweetened and embellished religion will ever be a favorite religious work, he wrote. But those who know that simple plainness and purity best suit the teachings of Christ look with horror on Milton's "wild and most ill conceived poetical romance."[51] In his diatribe against Milton, Roberts made use of all the common complaints habitually used by the Tories against the poet. "Milton's great failings (I judge from admitted facts) were a bad temper, a high opinion of himself, with inflexible obstinacy. He appears to have cared little for anyone but himself."[52] According to Roberts, Milton, of course, was whipped at Cambridge, mistreated Mary Powell, received "confidential and lucrative situations" under Cromwell, was imprisoned after the Civil War, and later published *Paradise Lost* which is nothing but "a few lines of spiritual truths . . . among an immense mass of impious fabrications."[53]

Another way which Milton's most vociferous opponents had
of ridiculing his political and religious views is evident in a
statement of the Reverend J. J. Blunt, who, in a review of
Milton's long-lost *De Doctrina Christiana,* which was redis-
covered in 1823, declared that the political and religious ideas
of Milton were wholly visionary and totally impractical.[54] According to Blunt, Milton was primarily a poet and dreamer,
and when he descended into the realm of practical matters, he
was a clown and a fool. The *De Doctrina,* he believed, had
made the visionary side of Milton even clearer. But it also had
an unfortunate effect. "The Politics of Milton," he wrote in
1827, "had been consigned to oblivion by common consent,
until recent circumstances [the publication of the *De Doctrina*
in 1825] accidentally revived them; and now to oblivion they
had better return—they are his 'uncomely parts.' Of his poetry,
it would require a tongue like his own to speak the praise. . . ."[55]
At the time, of course, Blunt could not foresee the great revival
of Milton's prose during the next decade—the prose which
with good reason the Tories had long despised. As the Reverend
W. L. Bowles stated in 1830, "I believe, the great talents, the
learning, the blameless lives, the powerful arguments, of Usher
and Hall, would have preserved the Church, if Milton had not
descended, with all his overwhelming might, of learning, eloquence, and scorn, into the contest." Indeed, it was Bowles's
opinion that it was Milton who suggested that Charles I's death
be made a *Grande Spectaculum* of national justice.[56]

The image of Milton as the stern Puritan was also given
wide currency by many important critics who had no desire
whatsoever to slander Milton, but who honestly felt that he
was unfortunately a Puritan. Matthew Arnold, who is typical
of this group, stated this attitude precisely when he wrote: "If
there is a defect which, above all others, is signal in Milton,
which injures him even intellectually, which limits him as a
poet, it is the defect common to him with the whole Puritan
party to which he belonged,—the fatal defect of *temper.* He

and they may have a thousand merits, but they are *unamiable.*
Excuse them how one will, Milton's asperity and acerbity, his
want of sweetness of temper, of the Shakespearian largeness
and indulgence, are undeniable."[57] Not only was Milton unamiable to some Victorians, he was, in their view, actually
unnatural. His coldness and austerity and lack of ordinary affections were too extreme to be normal. "From what we know of
Milton's character," Henry Stebbing remarked, "there is reason
to think that the ordinary passions of our nature were, from the
first dawn of manhood, subdued in his bosom. There was a
calmness and tranquility, amounting to sternness, in his conduct
and demeanour. . . . Love of woman never warmed him sufficiently to make him for a moment forget the severe assertion
of authority, and in his character of child and father no melting
tenderness, no irresistible flow of domestic joy, entered into its
composition." In Stebbing's opinion, Milton's "deficiency of
passion was the only element which was wanting to the perfection of his poetic character."[58]

Perhaps, however, the most interesting example of this attitude is found in Walter Bagehot's essay on Milton which
appeared in 1859. Here Bagehot attempted a kind of psycho-
logical analysis of Milton's character based on the premise that
there were two kinds of goodness conspicuous in the world,
sensuous and ascetic. Milton, of course, was the perfect example
of ascetic goodness, and Shakespeare was the exemplar of the
sensuous. Naturally introspective and idealistic, Milton, who
recognized his superior intellect and talents and delighted in
his own thoughts and imagination, soon withdrew himself from
the normal world of everyday affairs. This ascetic isolation, according to Bagehot, inevitably gave Milton a certain pride in
himself and an inevitable ignorance of others. Hence, he exhibited the usual faults of the ascetic type, pride and an unsympathetic character. In addition, this austerity was aided by
Milton's studious life and love of books and aggravated by "a
deficiency in humour, and a deficiency in a knowledge of plain
human nature."[59] Milton, furthermore, like all men of similar

constitution, soon realized that being aloof from others made him painfully unlike most people. Thus his "protective instinct" caused him to "recoil from the world, be offended at its amusements, be repelled by its occupations, be scared by its sins," and secluded him "in a sort of natural monastery." Afraid that his readers might feel that he had been "over-ready with depreciation or objection," Bagehot declared that in order to paint a likeness of the Puritan poet, it was necessary "that the harsher features of the subject should have a prominence."[60]

It is interesting that Bagehot and others of his persuasion used as their "text" the words reported by Jonathan Richardson in his *Explanatory Notes* to the effect that Milton "had a Gravity in his Temper, Not Melancholy, or not 'til the Latter Part of his Life, not Sour, Morose, or Ill-Natur'd; but a Certain Severity of Mind, a Mind not Condescending to Little Things."[61] The word "sour" for instance, recurs time and again in nineteenth-century discussions of Milton and the Puritans, and, coupled with "unamiable," in many ways sums up the dominant attitude toward Milton the Puritan.

Appealing to Richardson's quotation and "Milton's contemporaries," John Tulloch, an important Victorian authority on Puritanism, sought to support his conclusions about Milton. Like Bagehot, he believed that there were "two great types of human character, the broad, humane, and sympathetic, and the narrow, concentrated, and sustained." Milton, he said, belonged to the latter group. "His greatness awes us more than it delights us. It is like an isolated, solitary, and majestic eminence, which we never approach without reverence, but beneath the shadow of which few men dwell familiarly." Tulloch was able to admire Milton's loftiness, purity, and honesty, but he had to admit that his very goodness was not attractive. "It wants ease," he concluded; it lacks "freedom, and sweetness, and, above all, breadth and life of sympathy. It is cold, if not stern, in its severe harmony and goodness. His goodness is almost more stoical than Christian in its proud, self-sustained, and scornful strength."[62]

Not only was Milton, in the eyes of Bagehot and Tulloch, unsympathetic and cold, he was also dogmatic and narrow. Here, again, they felt, he had unfortunately been hampered by Puritanism. Tulloch pointed out that Puritanism itself was in many ways a very limited yet very confident and unyielding phase of thought. "In Milton," he continued, "it loses its limits, but it retains all its confidence and stubbornness. It soars, but it does not widen; and even in its highest flights it remains as ever essentially unsympathetic, scornful, and affirmative. It is positive, legislative, and authoritative. This is the temper of our author everywhere, and this was the Puritanical temper in its innermost expression."[63]

As I have shown, several important critics, free from the extreme prejudices of many writers with strong royalist and High Church sympathies, looked upon Milton's Puritanical characteristics with dissatisfaction. As Arnold expressed it, the advocates of the Puritans often boast that they produced Milton, our great epic poet, but "Alas! one might not unjustly retort that they spoiled him. However," said Arnold, "let Milton bear his own burden; in his temper he had natural affinities with the Puritans. He has paid for it by limitations as a poet."[64]

Although Puritanism in Arnold's opinion limited Milton's greatness, other commentators felt that the poet's connection with the Puritans reinforced those qualities one might properly expect to find in a great religious poet and prophet. David Masson, Milton's great biographer, had essentially this view. To Masson, Milton was a Puritan whose sternness, austerity and aloofness were a part of his nature from birth. But there was nothing unfortunate about this. Seriousness, "seriousness," Masson repeated, "a solemn and even austere demeanour of mind, was the characteristic of Milton even in his youth."[65] The controlling image of Milton in Masson's mind was that of a great religious poet who pre-eminently possesses and displays those qualities and characteristics of Homer, Virgil, and Dante in their role of *vates*. Milton was, as a man of his stature and vocation should have been, stern, aloof, magnificently dignified, and filled with the seriousmindedness of a great genius dedicated to the service of God. "A mind so constructed, so equipped, so nurtured," wrote one author, "could move only in a kindred sphere—apart from the littleness and petty conventionalities of thought and life. Hence the majestic solemnity, the moral austerity, and the colossal scale of all Milton's intellectual manifestations."[66]

George Gilfillan declared with approval that Milton alone "acted as well as wrote an epic complete in all its parts—high, grave, sustained, majestic." But earlier, in his *Life of Schiller,* Thomas Carlyle had already recalled Milton's belief that "he who would not be frustrate of his hope to write well hereafter in laudable things, ought himself to be a true poem; that is a composition and pattern of the best and honorablest things." To Carlyle, Milton was "the moral King of authors."[67] Perhaps this view of Milton can best be summed up in the remark that Milton stands before us "as the type of *Puritanism,* in its noblest development, retaining all its stern virtue and passionate devotion, but without its coarseness, its intolerance, or its stoicism."[68]

From three different points of view which persisted throughout the nineteenth century, Milton, as I have shown, was a stern Puritan. But it was perhaps David Masson and to a lesser extent Matthew Arnold who were more responsible than any others for the dominant late Victorian view of the stern, austere Milton.

III   Although Milton, the stern Puritan, was perhaps the dominant Victorian view, there were a number of critics who took a more historically correct, less biased position toward Milton and the Puritans. Certainly it would be a mistake to think that all Victorians considered all Puritans to be Mr. Chadbands, for, at times, Victorian critics attempted to correct the readers' uncritical image of Puritanism.

In his discussion of Masson's *Life of Milton,* one author addressed himself to what he described to be "current mistakes as regards the Puritans generally and Milton in particular." He believed that his fellows too commonly assumed that the Puritans were, "without exception, sour, splenetic, or fierce enthusiasts," and that Milton was of "the strictest sort among them, a Pharisee of the Pharisees." To the Puritans, he continued, "have been ascribed many of the extravagancies of other sectaries of the time, among whom the only feature in common was aversion to the ritual of the Church of England, as it was expounded and enforced by Laud and the high Arminian divines." The common view of Puritanism is, he remarked, incorrect. Puritans "disdained neither learning nor the arts." Furthermore, he concluded, it is incorrect to "impute to the Puritanism of the sixteenth and seventeenth centuries a universal spirit of gloom and asceticism."[69]

Tulloch, moreover, denied that Milton was a Puritan in its narrow, exaggerated sense, but he was not prepared, and rightly so, to agree with Macaulay that Milton was not a Puritan. "If by a Puritan," Tulloch wrote, Macaulay "meant one who wore long hair, who disliked music, who despised poetry, then Milton certainly was no Puritan. But," he pointed out, "it is only to a very material fancy that such qualities could be supposed to constitute Puritanism."[70] Similarly, Edward Dowden knew that the Victorians were usually acquainted "through the caricatures of dramatists and novelists" with the grotesque side of Puritan manners and morals—"the affectations of the precisian, the scruples with regard to things innocent, the casuistry by which self-indulgence was sanctified, the Hebraic phraseology, the danger of moroseness of temper." But he was careful to indicate that among the Puritans "were not a few men and women who added to purity of morals and the happiness of domestic affections, guarded as sacred, the best graces of culture and refinement."[71]

Various writers throughout the century were quick to declare that if Milton were a Puritan at all, it was in a very special and restricted sense. Edmonds made this clear when in the preface of his *Life* he said,

Milton, unequalled as a poet, and memorable and exemplary as a statesman, was most especially a Nonconformist, an advocate of religious freedom, unshackled by secular and political interference; —in a word, a Puritan, in all but those excesses of untempered zeal which historians and satirists have combined to exaggerate, in order to dim the historic lustre they cannot hide, and to throw contempt on a cause which must rise proportionately with the elevation and advancement of mankind.[72]

And Masson, while stating that the formation of Milton's character was aided "expressly and purposely by Puritanical influences," nevertheless went on to say that Milton could hardly be called a Puritan "in a denominational sense."[73] As Keightly phrased it, Milton was "brought up in Puritanism, but certainly not in 'the most straitest sect.' "[74]

This tendency to speak of Milton the Puritan with considerable reservation is illustrated, also, at the beginning of Tulloch's essay on Milton in *English Puritanism and Its Leaders.* "It may seem questionable," he wrote, "to assume Milton as a representative of Puritanism; and in the narrower sense of that word, the question would be a fair one; for Milton was certainly a great deal more than a Puritan. His mind and culture show elements even anti-Puritan."[75] Often the writers who saw how un-Puritan Milton was in many respects gave considerable emphasis to his early years—his love of music, the Latin poets and the theatre; his calm and peaceful life at Horton, and his grand tour on the Continent—and occasionally stressed his late views, especially his Arianism, latitudinarian practices, and the fact that he "owned no church." Dowden made a point of the fact that Milton, unlike Bunyan—and many a Victorian—never experienced the agonies of hope and fear, the terrors of hell, the despair of the unsaved. "From his earliest years," wrote Dowden, "Milton toiled steadily, as under a great task-master's eye; his higher life was not like Bunyan's, the outcome of a conversion; it was rather a going-on towards perfection."[76]

Although the Reverend J. J. Blunt still believed the Puritans to be generally a bad lot, to him Milton was a "magnificent specimen of the Puritan in his least offensive form." Milton was in his fervor, devotion, honest indignation, moral fearlessness, uncompromising impetuosity, and fantastic imagination, a Puritan, but these laudable traits were, in Blunt's opinion, unalloyed "by the hypocrisy, the vulgarity, the cant, the cunning, and bad taste which have so generally made the name to stink in the nostrils of men."[77]

Certainly one of the most common ideas about Puritanism that had existed from the seventeenth century onward was the belief in the minds of many that the Puritans hated great art and destroyed the English theatre, and we can see this attitude very clearly expressed in William Gifford's preface to *The Plays of Massinger,* which appeared in 1813. When the government of Charles I fell, he wrote, "a set of austere and gloomy fanatics, enemies to every elegant amusement, and every social relaxation, rose upon the ruins of the state. Exasperated by the ridicule with which they had long been covered by the stage, they persecuted the actors with unrelenting severity, and consigned them, together with the writers, to hopeless obscurity and wretchedness." Moreover, Gifford believed that England had not yet recovered from the catastrophe which this struggle brought upon the fine arts which, he declared, were, at the time of the Civil War, rapidly advancing to perfection "under the fostering wing of a monarch who united in himself, taste to feel, spirit to undertake, and munificence to reward."[78]

However, some years later, Charles Kingsley returned to this particular passage in Gifford's preface for the express purpose of showing how false this view of English art was. Admitting that "a great part" of his own generation shared Gifford's notion, Kingsley in his volume *Plays and Puritans* attempted to correct a false and somewhat malicious idea.[79] Kingsley first pointed out that the English stage had soon after Shakespeare's death declined into "perversity and mediocrity." Furthermore, the Anglicans had along with the Puritans attacked the licentiousness of the stage for years. Besides this, he felt, the Puritan attitude was perfectly right in opposing plays which laughed at and made comedy of adultery, prostitution, and every form of fraud and hypocrisy. Of course, the Puritans, he continued, hated bad, immoral art, but, like Milton, they were no rigid haters of the beautiful. Using Milton as his example, Kingsley wrote that the poet had "steeped his whole soul in romance" and had "felt the beauty and glory of the chivalrous Middle Age as deeply as Shakespeare himself." Milton felt, he remarked, "to his heart's core . . . the magnificence and worth of really high art, of the drama when it was worthy of man and itself." Kingsley was of the opinion that perhaps no poet "shows wider and truer sympathy with every form of the really beautiful in art, nature, and history" than does Milton. However, he concluded, despite all this sympathy for great art, Milton was a Puritan. "Yes, Milton was a Puritan, one, who instead of trusting himself and his hopes of the universe to second-hand hearsays, systems, and traditions, had looked God's Word and his own soul in the face, and determined to act on that which he had found."[80]

In combatting the notion that Milton was a stern Puritan of "the most straitest sect," Victorian critics often noticed Milton's independence of mind and spirit and his penchant for finding his own solutions to problems and following through the logical consequences of his ideas. He was, they sought to make known, no narrow sectarian. Neither in religion nor politics, they noticed, was he a prey to thoughtless partisanship or blind devotion to a party. Milton was "a freethinker in the highest and best sense of the term," said Richard Garnett;[81] and F. D. Maurice remarked that Milton dwelt apart from the factions of his age when he was in the midst of faction: "The party he is fighting for," Maurice continued, "is dear to him only for the sake of the purpose to which he supposes that it is pledged."[82] In addition, it was Dowden's opinion that Milton's theology and philosophy were "akin in some respects to the Puritanism of his time," yet they were independent and "identical with no current doctrine."[83] To be sure, after the appearance of the *De Doctrina* it was more difficult to think of Milton as a narrow sectarian, and yet the idea persisted on a wide scale. But certainly the latitudinarian tone and Milton's ideas concerning polygamy and the Sabbath which are expressed in the *De Doctrina* were un-Puritan as Tulloch pointed out. They are, in reality, he said, "the natural development of that spirit of free-thinking which, in Milton as in some others, struggled all along with the dogmatism of their time."[84]

Just as Jonathan Richardson's report that Milton was sour and morose was often quoted by the advocates of the stern Puritanical Milton, so Richardson's report that he was "Delightful Company, the Life of the Conversation," was frequently repeated by those who believed that Milton was a man of normal sensibilities.[85] Raleigh flatly stated that Milton was not, as he had sometimes been described, "a callous and morose Puritan." On the contrary, "He was extraordinarily susceptible to the attractions of feminine beauty and grace."[86] This, too, had been the opinion of Mrs. Jameson who had early declared that Milton had a passionate, congenial character. In *Memoirs of the Loves of the Poets,* she wrote that Milton, "whose harmonious soul was tuned to the music of the spheres," has left us "the most exquisite pictures of tenderness and beauty—to think of such a being as a petty domestic tyrant, a coarse-minded fanatic, stern and unfeeling in all the relations of life, were enough to confound all our ideas of moral fitness."[87] It was Richard Garnett's belief that Milton was a sensitive man with all the "impulsive passion of the poetical temperament," despite the fact that most Victorians thought of him as a "great, good, reverend, austere, not very amiable, and not very sensitive man."[88]

In fact, several critics went so far as to believe that in many ways Milton was not narrow by any stretch of the imagination, but rather as many-sided and as representative of the English spirit as Shakespeare was. "More even than Shakespeare, if I may dare say so," wrote John Robert Seeley, "[Milton] enlarges our conception of our national character."[89] And George Gilfillan similarly declared that it was Milton, "not Goethe or Shakspeare," who seems to us "the many-sided man of the

modern world. He was complete in all powers and accomplish-
ments, almost as his own Adam. He had every faculty both of
body and of mind, well-developed and finely harmonised."[90]

IV   Seeley and Gilfillan were not alone in seeing
                a Milton of varied talents and seemingly
contradictory qualities and tendencies. Many people who have
studied Milton have known that he cannot be explained simply
in terms of Puritanism or humanism or republicanism. He was
the last of the great Renaissance figures, yet he was an equally
great Puritan spirit; he did have many aristocratic tastes, but
he fully supported a republican cause. As Edmond Scherer wrote
in his famous essay, Milton "is an elegant poet and a passionate
controversialist, an accomplished humanist and a narrow sec-
tary"; he was "never exactly a Prynne or exactly a Petrarch."[91]
And during the Victorian period, Milton's varied qualities of
mind and art were dramatically illustrated by a century-long debate over his poetic nature which, as I shall show, was closely
related to the widespread view that as a youthful poet, Milton
was a genial, cultivated man of the Renaissance who, during the
Civil War years, gradually changed into a harsh and aloof poet
filled with the austere spirit of Puritanism.

To David Masson, this Renaissance-Puritan view of Milton
was not congenial, because he firmly believed that Milton was
from beginning to end a Puritan by nature. "Underneath the
flowers and the beauty" of the early poems, Masson saw the
austere and disciplined character of the Puritan spirit. Consequently, he was certain that Milton was an exception to the
dominant notion that the poetic nature is marked by spontaneity
and impulsiveness, pure sensibility and a desire for strong pleas-
urable emotion unguarded by principle and discipline. Yet E. S.
Dallas, in *The Gay Science,* heartily disagreed with Masson on
this point. In Dallas' mind, Milton, like Carlyle's heroes, could
have won fame in any field. True, he chose to be a poet, but
he was more. "He was a statesman—but he was more. He was
a great religious thinker and worker—but again he was more.

He was one of the most learned men of his time, he was certainly the most accomplished, he was perhaps the most masterly, Latin writer since the classical age had passed away. To state the matter shortly—he was the most complete man to be found in his day. . . . In what other character," asked Dallas, "can we find such an astonishing assemblage of qualities and sympathies, many of them apparently opposite; austerity combined with sensibility, rare tolerance combined with thought, poetry combined with politics, purity combined with passion, piety combined with the fullest enjoyment of earth?"[92]

So far as Dallas was concerned, Milton had not been devoid of poetic sensibility as a young man, nor had what Masson called "that native austerity of feeling and temper, that real though not formal Puritanism of heart and intellect" stifled the spontaneity and emotional response of Milton's truly poetical temperament. Masson, he felt, had "overrated the want of sensibility and the amount of principle in Milton's youthful character. . . . What, after all," Dallas continued, "can we trace in Milton's youth except beautiful sensibility, enormous intellectual voracity, intense enjoyment of study and of all things good and fair?" In Milton's early poems Dallas was able to find no dogmatic assertion. On the contrary, the early poems were written when Milton was in "that stage of pure sensibility, when he seems to be ready for all moods alike, provided they are beautiful; he is willing to assume any premises, and then on the strength of them to give his imagination free play for the mere pleasure of the emotion."[93]

But, in contrast, Dallas noticed that Milton's later poems were separated in spirit—"I might say, by the whole diameter of feeling—" from these early poems.[94] In other words, Milton's character and art both changed radically—at least in spirit—at some point during his life. And in this, Dallas illustrates yet another aspect of the Victorian attitude toward Milton, the Puritan, which was held by many who, like Coleridge, believed that the best way to explain the seemingly disparate elements in Milton's character and art was to approach them biographically by showing that the poet grew to manhood when the spirit of the Renaissance, the temper of the Elizabethan age, was yet dominant, and that his mature years, however, were spent in a different world, a world of Puritan austerity and civil strife.

Although critics such as Masson and Tulloch saw the cold pure light of the stern Puritan temperament shining through the earliest poems of Milton, many emphasized a Milton whose life clearly fell into three periods: a youthful period from 1608 to about 1639 when the poet was a graceful, talented man filled with the spirit of the Renaissance; the middle years when Milton was swept into a Puritan world of political and religious controversy; and the final period when the blind poet consoled himself and expressed his frustrated desires in his great poems, *Paradise Lost, Paradise Regained,* and *Samson Agonistes.* F. D. Maurice, for example, was convinced that one "cannot understand him [Milton], or his works, in any way so well as by connecting them with the stages of his life. . . . The verse and prose of Milton, far more than those of most great men, are expressive of what he was doing, enjoying, or suffering at the time they were poured out."[95]

The "three periods" approach to Milton, so common in Victorian criticism, was perhaps best exemplified in Mark Pattison's popular short life of Milton in which he pointed out that

> Milton's life is a drama in three acts. The first discovers him in the calm and peaceful retirement of Horton, of which *L'Allegro, Il Penseroso,* and *Lycidas* are the expression. In the second act he is breathing the foul and heated atmosphere of party passion and religious hate, generating the lurid fires which glare in the battailous canticles of his prose pamphlets. The three great poems, *Paradise Lost, Paradise Regained,* and *Samson Agonistes,* are the utterance of his final period of solitary Promethean grandeur, when, blind, destitute, friendless, he testified of righteousness, temperance, and judgment to come, alone before a fallen world.[96]

It was in *Lycidas* that Pattison detected the first shadows of the stern Puritan Milton stealing across the sunny pastoral landscape of the early poems. "Milton's original picturesque vein," he wrote, is in *Lycidas* crossed for the first time

with one of quite another sort. . . . The fanaticism of the cove-
nanter and the sad grace of Petrarch seem to meet in Milton's
monody. . . . The conflict between the old cavalier world—the years
of gaiety and festivity of a splendid and pleasure loving court, and
the new puritan world into which love and pleasure were not to
enter—this conflict which was commencing in the social life of
England, is also begun in Milton's own breast, and is reflected in
Lycidas.[97]

The two Miltons, the Renaissance, Elizabethan, Cavalier
Milton and the Puritan poet and polemicist—these stood out in
sharp contrast in the minds of many Victorians. Matthew
Arnold agreed with Edmond Scherer that from the first "two
conflicting forces, two sources of inspiration, had contended with
one another . . . for the possession of Milton,—the Renascence
and Puritanism."[98] Critics, too, were aware that in his poetry,
Milton had succeeded in reconciling and blending "the genius
of pagan art and beauty with the genius of the Christian religion." Milton demonstrated, said Courthope, "that in the true
spirit of the Renaissance there was nothing essentially antago-
nistic to the spirit of the reformation."[99] Thus, the advocates of
the Renaissance-Puritan Milton and the "three periods" approach warned their public not to read into Milton's early life
the later attitudes and character of the poet. Those who see
nothing in the child Milton, "but the bearded gloom of the
Regicide and the full-grown asceticism of the Puritan," were,
in the opinion of Arthur Windsor, letting their imagination
run away with them.[100]

Of course, the great change in Milton's disposition was, of
necessity, attributed to the middle period of his life when he
immersed himself in the defense of the Commonwealth and
the reformed churches. As a result, many including Pattison
lamented the years in which—according to them—Milton prosti-
tuted his talents, devoted himself to scurrilous prose and turned
his back on poetry. Egerton Brydges' comment is quite typical
of those who eschewed Milton the prose writer, the political and
religious thinker, who allowed bitter controversy to destroy the
grand promise of his earlier poetic years. According to Brydges,

"Milton's evil days began" as soon as he returned from the Continent. "He entered into thorny controversies which blind the imagination, and harden and embitter the heart. It was not for sublime talents, like his, to entangle themselves in these webs."[101]

But others defended Milton's decision to enter the political arena, and believed that instead of injuring his poetic career, it was, on the contrary, a benefit. "If Milton had sequestered himself in the culture of the beautiful," said Peter Bayne, "when duty called him to the service of his country, he would never have been one of the poets of the world. We might have had from him a miracle of learning and elaboration, 'pencilled over,' to use his own language, 'with all the curious touches of art, even to the perfection of a faultless picture'; but," he continued, "the inspiration of a great time would not have thrilled through it with the modulation of the long-rolling thunder peal, nor would it have taught many generations how lofty was the enthusiasm, how mighty the fervour, that dwelt in the Puritans of England."[102]

Raleigh, who admitted that the English people had a deep-rooted prejudice against poets who concern themselves intimately with politics, stoutly defended Milton against this prejudice and mockingly parodied Pattison and others when he wrote, "But what was Milton doing in this malodorous and noisy assembly? Might he not with all confidence have left the Church to the oyster-women, and the state to the mouse-trap men?"[103]

Regardless, however, of how one viewed Milton's middle years, all agreed that the poet changed; and whether a person believed with Masson that during the war years Milton's true, austere nature asserted itself, or whether one followed Dallas in believing that the poet's character more radically altered, most people were quite aware that sooner or later the Renaissance elements and the Elizabethan spirit in Milton were overcome and subordinated to the Puritanical qualities of his nature. As Edward Dowden expressed it, "Milton was essentially a Puritan. In spite of his classical culture, and his Renaissance

sense of beauty, he not less than Bunyan saw, as the prime fact
of the world, Diabolus at odds with Immanuel."[104] And Masson's years of arduous study led him to conclude that Milton
"most truly and properly" belonged to "the great Puritan body
of his countrymen. . . . Only an unscholarly misconception of
Puritanism, a total ignorance of the actual facts of its history,
will ever seek, now or henceforward, to rob English Puritanism
of Milton, or Milton of his title to be remembered as the genius
of Puritan England."[105]

VI ✍ Milton and Tennyson

This is an art
Which does mend Nature, change it rather, but
The art itself is Nature.
—The Winter's Tale, IV, iv, 95–97

I   Of the five major Victorian poets, Alfred Tennyson was most influenced by Milton. Tennyson's use of Miltonic elements in his sonnets has already been discussed and the young poet, experimenting in verse throughout the 1820's, was aware, like Montgomery and Heraud, of the natural Sublime in Milton's epics. However, it was neither Milton's use of the sonnet nor the Sublime in his poetry which primarily interested Tennyson. The attraction, in fact, was of a much more subtle and fundamental kind; it was the attraction which one congenial mind has for another—a meeting of two minds which considered the true poet to be both artist and seer.

Since Tennyson was so convinced that the great poet must be a consummate artist as well as an inspired teacher, it is no surprise that Milton and Virgil were his favorite poets, whom he honored and emulated throughout his entire life. To each he dedicated a poem of praise which brings together the essence of his opinion and focus of his esteem. Milton, the "mighty-mouth'd inventor of harmonies," the "God-gifted organ-voice of England"; Milton, the poet who could paint idyllic Eden in all its mystery and richness: this was the artist who attracted Tennyson. Similarly, it was Virgil, the "Landscape-lover," the "Lord of language," Virgil of the "golden phases," the wielder of the "stateliest measure ever molded by the lips of man," that appealed most to Tennyson. Milton was the most sublime of all poets; *Lycidas,* the touchstone of poetic taste,[1] and when the Laureate thought of the "grand style" of poetic diction, the supreme two were Milton and Virgil.[2]

Tennyson's love for Milton and Virgil and his desire to emulate them came from the fact that they were kindred spirits —men who from birth were dedicated to the task of making the most of their God-given talents. Fully aware of their "ethereal origin and celestial descent,"[3] fully cognizant that their abilities were "the inspiried gift of God rarely bestowed,"[4] these men knew that their task demanded the utmost consecration to the ideals of virtue, truth, and beauty. Moreover, they knew that their abilities were "of power beside the office of a pulpit, to imbreed and cherish in a great people the seeds of virtue and public civility, to allay the perturbations of the mind and set the affections in right tune, . . . to deplore the general relapses of kingdoms and state from justice and God's true worship."[5] Finally, they knew that their lives must conform to the ideal pattern of the inspired artist.

To Virgil, Milton, and Tennyson, the ideal poet will concern himself in youth with the simpler, less arduous art of pastoral poetry, and will (in Tennyson's words) follow the sweet magic of the poetic imagination "over the valley, / In early summers, / Over the mountain," and will sing of pastoral matters:

> Pasture and plowland,
> Innocent maidens,
> Garrulous children,
> Homestead and harvest,
> Reaper and gleaner,
> And rough-ruddy faces
> Of lowly labor,

but finally the day comes when the song of the true poet must be "stronger and statelier," it must lead "to the city and palace,"[6] and ultimately it must pass through all the experiences of the human race. As Milton had said, the poet must take leave of the "smooth elegiacs"[7] and pastorals forever, for he must turn his thoughts and talents toward a work "doctrinal and exemplary to a nation,"[8] he must sing of "wars and heavens," he must tell of the "sacred counsels of the gods on high."[9] Not only must his youth "be innocent of crime and chaste, his conduct irreproachable and his hands stainless,"[10] but his original gift of genius must be combined with and tempered by the "learned pains." Milton knew that his work could be achieved only by "labor and intent study . . . joined with the strong propensity of nature."[11]

The poetry of Tennyson shows that he entirely agreed with Milton and Virgil, who had no illusions about "unpremeditated art." Constant and laborious effort alone bring each utterance to full perfection. " '*Poeta nascitur non fit*' indeed, 'Poeta nascitur et fit,' " said Tennyson. By the age of twelve, young Alfred was running about the fields of Somersby shouting scraps of epic poetry and feeling mightily inspired, but later the mature poet said, "I suppose I was nearer thirty than twenty before I was anything of an artist."[12] Speaking of Milton and Tennyson, Frederic Harrison once commented that "in the whole range of English poetry, Milton alone can be held to show an equal or even greater uniformity of polish than Tennyson."[13] The stanzas of *In Memoriam* are "after Milton's the most faultlessly chiseled verse in our language."[14]

Tennyson probably never knew when he first became aware of Milton, because it is obvious from the records of life at Somersby that the author of *Paradise Lost* was one of the household poets who was constantly referred to, spoken of, and read. Alfred Tennyson's father, the Reverend Dr. George Clayton Tennyson, rector of Somersby, was a well-educated man who loved and wrote poetry and was a connoisseur of good books. He brought together a rather extensive library of the best authors so that his sons would have the advantage of reading the great literature of the world, even though they lived in rural and remote Lincolnshire. The size and scope of his collection can be surmised by various reports of the boys' reading. "Amongst the authors most read by them were Shakespeare, Milton, Burke, Goldsmith, Rabelais, Sir William Jones, Addison, Swift, Defoe, Cervantes, Bunyan and Buffon";[15] and Tennyson and his brothers "became familiar with Spenser, Shakespeare, Beaumont and Fletcher, Milton, Pope, Thomson, Collins, Gray, Campbell, Macpherson's *Ossian,* Byron and Scott."[16] One of the gifts which Tennyson prized throughout his life was a second edition of *Paradise Lost* which his father gave him, at the age of seven, when he went away to school at Louth.[17]

Milton, of course, is mentioned in both the above lists, but a fuller and more interesting example of Alfred's acquaintance with Milton is found in his earliest extant letter, which the twelve-year-old wrote to his Aunt Marianne in order to instruct her in the prosody of "Sampson Agonistes."[18] The task was evidently a difficult one for a boy of twelve, but fortunately a copy of Bishop Newton's famous life with his extensive notes to the poems was in the library. "Going into the library this morning," wrote Alfred, "I picked up 'Sampson Agonistes' on which (as I think it is a play you like) I shall send you my remarks." His "remarks" include quotations of "particularly beautiful" passages such as the one on Samson's blindness, "O dark, dark, dark, amid the blaze of noon." He also noted Newton's explanation of the word "diffused" and pointed out to his aunt that the metre of the chorus is taken from the Greek. Even at this early age, Tennyson was interested in Milton's use of language; for instance, he noticed the expression "the Gates of Azzar" and wrote: "this probably, as Bp. Newton observes, was to avoid too great an alliteration, which the 'Gates of Gaza' would have caused, though (in my opinion) it would have rendered it more beautiful: and (though I do not affirm it as a fact) perhaps Milton gave it that name for the sake of novelty, as all the world knows he was a great pedant."[19]

But what does the poetry of this early period tell us about Tennyson's feelings for Milton? Certainly the early work of Tennyson's apprenticeship shows, as does the early work of any good poet, that he was imitating a rather wide range of models. Just as Milton studied Ovid, Petrarch, and Spenser, so Tennyson imitated the Elizabethans, Milton, Pope, and the late eighteenth- and early nineteenth-century poets.[20] Consequently his attitude toward Milton, especially in those early years, can best be ascertained by tracing Miltonic influence on the poems through the 1827 volume of *Poems by Two Brothers*. Although the young poet tended to go through "Scott phases," "Miltonic phases," and Byronic moods, the influence of Milton appears to have been steadier and more enduring than that of any other poet. For instance, the blank verse play, *The Devil and the Lady,* written when Alfred was about fourteen, includes "plentiful echoes of Milton";[21] and "Armageddon" is "strictly Miltonic, both in subject and in technique."[22] Although many of Alfred's contributions to *Poems by Two Brothers* are imitative of the fashionable poetry of the time—Gray, Byron, Moore, and Scott,[23] quotations, echoes, and imitations of Milton are found throughout.

"Armageddon," however, is by far the most important Miltonic poem in the pre-Cambridge period. Written when Tennyson was "not more than fifteen,"[24] it shows clearly how familiar the young poet was with Milton's blank verse, diction, and subject matter. Later it was to serve as a basis for the prize poem, *Timbuctoo,* but a few lines survive which indicate that "Armageddon" itself was based on an earlier version which also was Miltonic as these two lines show:

> And shadowing forth th' unutterable tomb,
> Making a 'darkness visible.'[25]

Not wholly unlike the "apocalyptic" poems of the 1820's, it opens with the poet standing upon a mountain overlooking "the valley of Megiddo."[26] The sun sets with "portentous glare":

Strange figures thickly thronged his burning orb
Spirits of discord seemed to weave across
His fiery disk a web of bloody haze,
Through whose reticulations struggled forth
His ineffectual, intercepted beams
Curtaining in one dark terrific pall
Of dun-red light heaven's azure and earth's green.

Then comes the "rustling of white wings"; a young seraph appears who frees the poet's vision from the fetters of mortality; his "mental eye" grows large, and he seems "to stand / Upon the outward verge and bound alone / Of God's omniscience." He sees "The Moon's white cities. . . . And notes of busy life in distant worlds, / Beat, like a far wave" on his anxious ear:

Highly and holily the Angel look'd.
Immeasurable Solicitude and Awe,
And solemn Adoration and high Faith,
Were trac'd on his imperishable front—
Then with a mournful and ineffable smile,
Which but to look on for a moment fill'd
My eyes with irresistible sweet tears,
In accents of majectic melody,
Like a swollen river's gushings in still night
Mingled with floating music, thus he spoke.

"O Everlasting God, and thou not less
The Everlasting Man . . .
O Lords of Earth and Tyrannies of Hell,
And thrones of Heaven, whose triple pride shall clash
In the annihilating anarchy
Of unimaginable war, a day
Of darkness riseth on ye, a thick day,
Pall'd with dun wreaths of dusky flight, a day
Of many thunders and confused noise,
Of bloody grapplings in the interval
Of the opposed Battle, a great day
Of wonderful revealings and vast sights
And inconceivable visions, such as yet
Have never shone into the heart of Man—
The Day of the Lord God!" . . .

Nothing so obviously imitative of *Paradise Lost* is found among Alfred's poems in *Poems by Two Brothers;* nevertheless, "Persia" and the ode "On Sublimity" are notable for what Professor Lounsbury called "an almost Miltonic Wealth of nomenclature."[27] "Persia"[28] is prefaced by "The flower and choice / Of many provinces from bound to bound" (*Paradise Regained,* III, 314–15), and shows that Tennyson's love of beautiful words and phrases appeared early and fed itself upon the "mighty" lines and golden phrases of Marlowe and Milton. Exotic proper nouns are the *sine qua non* of this poem of geographic description which takes us from the blooming bowers "Of Schiraz or of Ispahan" through "high Persepolis of old" to

> hot Syene's wondrous well,
> Nigh to the long-liv'd Aethiops.
> And northward far to Trebizonde,
> Renown'd for kings of chivalry,
> Near where old Hyssus, from the strand,
> Disgorges in the Euxine sea—
> The Euxine, falsely nam'd, which whelms
> The mariner in the heaving tide,
> To high Sinope's distant realms,
> Whence cynics rail'd at human pride.

"On Sublimity"[29] takes the reader "by Teneriffe's peak, or Kilda's giant height," and we follow the poet, a latter-day Penseroso, as he wanders "at midnight alone"

> Through some august cathedral, where, from high,
> The cold, clear moon on the mosaic stone
> Comes glancing in gay colours gloriously,
> Through windows rich with gorgeous blazonry.

Prefaced, appropriately enough, by "Immutable—immortal —infinite!" (*Paradise Lost,* III, 373), "The Deity"[30] is reminiscent of Milton's description of "the glorious brightness" of God whose skirts appear "dark with excessive bright," for the glorious light of Tennyson's Deity is "insufferably bright," and He sits "Thron'd in sequester'd sanctity, / And with transcendent glories crown'd."

In November, 1827, Alfred and his brother Charles went up to Cambridge, and it was not long before Tennyson became intimate with the "Apostles," a group of highly promising young men who were "genial, high-spirited, poetical, . . . full of speculation and of enthusiasm for the great literature of the past, and for the modern schools of thought, and despised rhetoric and sentimentalism."[31] Among these were Arthur Hallam, Monckton Milnes, and James Spedding, who have left interesting comments on Milton which reflect the general opinion of the "Apostles." Although they were evidently interested in Wordsworth, Keats, and Shelley, Milton had a high place in their thought.

Hallam, for example, must like Tennyson have known Milton from childhood, since one of his early poems, "The Bride of the Lake," is "adorned with allusions to Dante and Milton."[32] Later he wrote his "Timbuctoo" in "scorn for anybody's opinion, who did not value Plato and Milton just as much as I did." And, as a result, he said, "I 'fit audience found tho' few!' "[33] In his discussions of Tennyson's art he often compared his friend's poetry with that of Milton. Speaking of the "Recollections of the Arabian Nights," he said: ". . . the concise boldness with which in a few words an object is clearly painted, is sometimes (see the 6th stanza) majestic as Milton."[34] In 1833 he wrote Tennyson in Somersby that "I hear to-day that a question is put up at the Cambridge Union, 'Tennyson or Milton, which is the greater poet.' "[35] But Hallam's most important opinion of Milton is found in his review of Sorelli's translation of *Paradise Lost* into Italian. He observed "the lavish riches of Milton's imagination," and went on to say that *Paradise Lost*

> stands before us like a perfect statue, in which the rich finish of the separate parts heightens rather than impairs the predominant expression of individual characters. . . . The deep harmonies of the *Paradise Lost* are beyond admiration as beyond measurement. . . . Not the metre merely, nor the pauses, nor the balanced numbers but every word, every syllable, every combination of vowels and consonants, appears the offspring of consummate art.[36]

When the young Monckton Milnes wanted to show how fine Tennyson's *Timbuctoo* was, he was somehow able to write that "Tennyson's poem has made quite a sensation; it is certainly equal to most parts of Milton."[37] And as late as 1834, James Spedding wrote Tennyson from Keswick, complaining that he has written very little verse because he has been too ambitious in trying to equal "Milton's high-learned manner."[38]

Poems, Chiefly Lyrical (1830) and *Poems* (1832) contain, along with a few other pieces excluded from these volumes, the work of the Cambridge period. This poetry is the last in which the direct influence of Milton can be observed. Here as in the pre-Cambridge poems, Milton's influence is very notable and adds, once again, to our knowledge, of Tennyson's attitude. For contrary to expectations, Tennyson drew far more heavily from "the older English poets, from Milton especially, and from Shakespeare, than from his immediate predecessors."[39] Speaking particularly of the Cambridge period, Professor J. F. A. Pyre concluded: "So thoroughly is [Tennyson's] verse suffused with the colors of Milton's descriptive poetry that the phrases actually taken by him direct from Milton only feebly illustrate the extent to which he has submitted his technique to the Miltonic discipline."[40]

For example, the tone and diction of the "Ode to Memory" are obviously derived from "Il Penseroso," which evidently affected Tennyson more profoundly than did its companion, "L'Allegro." Memory is invoked in much the same manner as Milton calls up "divinest Melancholy":

> Come forth, I charge thee, arise,
> Thou of the many tongues, the myriad eyes!
> Thou comest not with shows of flaunting vines
> Unto mine inner eye
> Divinest Memory!

But the ode concludes as it began in the Penseroso vein:

> My friend, with you to live alone
> Were how much better than to own
> A crown a sceptre and a throne!

In addition to this example of influence, there are three other pieces which are especially interesting in various ways. One is a "whimsical little poem," long unpublished, which shows again Tennyson's warm feeling toward Milton. "Milton's Mulberry,"[41] of course, recalls the Leonora legend noted earlier. The mulberry tree which Milton was presumed to have planted and under which Leonora was supposed to have found the poet asleep, was still a cherished memorial at Christ's College in 1830:

> Look what love the puddle-pated square-caps have for me.
> I am Milton's Mulberry, Milton's Milton's Mulberry,
> But they whip't and rusticated him who planted me
> Milton's, Milton's Mulberry, Milton's Milton's Mulberry!
> Old and hollow, somewhat crooked in the shoulders
>   as you see,
> Full of summer foliage yet but propped and padded
>   curiously,
> I would sooner have been planted by the hand that
>   planted me
> Than have grown in Paradise and dropped my fruit
>   on Adam's knee!
> Look what love the tiny witted Trenchers have for me.

The Cambridge prize poem of 1829, *Timbuctoo*,[42] represents not only the first published blank verse of Tennyson, but it is also the blank verse which most closely approximates that of *Paradise Lost*.[43] When Tennyson decided to enter the competition for the Chancellor's Medal, he sent home for the "Armageddon." As Charles Tennyson says, "only a small quantity of *Armageddon* was actually incorporated in it [*Timbuctoo*], though there is a similarity between the general framework of the poems. In each an angel comes down to the poet when standing on a mountain, but what the angel says and the poet sees necessarily differ in each."[44] Both poems, but especially the later one, indicate how carefully Tennyson studied and experimented with Milton's blank verse. The fact that he chose this verse form over the traditional heroic couplet in his attempt to win the coveted prize shows how much he admired the non-dramatic blank verse of *Paradise Lost*. A few lines and a verse paragraph of *Timbuctoo* will illustrate how thoroughly Tennyson had assimilated the characteristic qualities of Milton's verses at this date. In the two following quotations from the poem, note his manipulation of syntax, his deft handling of the long verse paragraph, his diction rich with proper nouns, his archaic spellings, and his use of repetition. This passage, for example, is quite Miltonic:

> Divinest Atalantis, whom the waves
> Have buried deep, and thou of later name,
> Imperial Eldorado, roof'd with gold.

When the poet at last beholds the city of Timbuctoo, he describes it in a manner not only highly reminiscent of Milton's handling of blank verse, but also in terms which recall Pandemonium as well as the "glistering Spires and Pinnacles" of Heaven as they appeared to Satan:[45]

> Then first within the south methought I saw
> A wilderness of spires, and chrystal pile
> Of rampart upon rampart, dome on dome,
> Illimitable range of battlement
> On battlement, and the imperial height
> Of canopy o'ercanopied . . .
>   But the glory of the place
> Stood out a pillar'd front of burnish'd gold,
> Interminably high, if gold it were
> Or metal more etherial, and beneath
> Two doors of blinding brilliance, where no gaze
> Might rest, stood open, and the eye could scan,
> Through length of porch and valve and boundless hall,
> Part of a throne of fiery flame, wherefrom
> The snowy skirting of a garment hung,
> And glimpse of multitudes of multitudes
> That minister'd around it—.

The last and by far the best poem to be mentioned is "The Hesperides," which was printed in the 1832 volume and then suppressed.[46] Just why a poem so metrically perfect and so magically beautiful as this one failed to be republished during the poet's lifetime is, indeed, a puzzle. Perhaps it was too purely a piece of art for art's sake, and too remote from the real life of men; but, at any rate, it is the best explanation of why in "Milton" Tennyson said:

> Me rather all that bowery loneliness,
> The brooks of Eden mazily murmuring,
>   And bloom profuse and cedar arches
>   Charm, as a wanderer out in ocean,
> Where some refulgent sunset of India
> Streams o'er a rich ambrosial ocean isle,
>   And crimson-hued the stately palm-woods
>   Whisper in odorous heights of even.

Milton's Eden and his "happy isles,"

> Like those Hesperian Gardens fam'd of old,
> Fortunate Fields, and Groves and flow'ry Vales,
> Thrice happy isles . . .
>
> *(Paradise Lost,* III, 567–69)

must have had a powerful effect on the young artist who, at times, longed for "the yellow down"

> Border'd with palm, and many a winding vale
> And meadow, set with slender galingale;
> A land where all things always seem'd the same!
>
> ("The Lotos-Eaters")

The fact that Milton could write an *Arcades* or a *Comus* with its Eden-like epilogue and a *Paradise Lost* which contains the most lovely descriptions of Paradise in all literature was never overlooked by Tennyson either early or late, for we know that the description of Eden in the fourth book of *Paradise Lost* was one of his favorite passages. Hallam Tennyson recalled that his father once quoted from memory the description of the garden beginning with "Flow'rs worthy of Paradise which not nice Art / In Beds and curious knots, but Nature boon / Pour'd forth profuse on Hill and Dale and Plain."[47] And Francis Palgrave, the poet's close friend, remembered that Tennyson

"specially singled out for delicate beauty" the Gate of Heaven
(*Paradise Lost,* III, 501–509, a passage which the poet knew
well when he wrote *Timbuctoo*) and "the great vision of Eden
[*Paradise Lost,* IV, 205-311], which he read aloud" with great
pleasure on various occasions. But Palgrave goes on to observe
that the poet dwelt "always on the peculiar grace"[48] of these
lines:

> Thus was this place,
> A happy rural seat of various view:
> Groves whose rich Trees wept odorous Gums and Balm,
> Others whose fruit burnisht with Golden Rind
> Hung amiable, *Hesperian* Fables true,
> If true, here only, and of delicious taste:
> Betwixt them Lawns, or level Downs, and Flocks
> Grazing the tender herb, were interpos'd,
> Or palmy hillock, or the flow'ry lap
> Of some irriguous Valley spread her store,
> Flow'rs of all hue, and without Thorne the Rose:
> Another side, umbrageous Grots and Caves
> Of cool recess, o'er which the mantling vine
> Lays forth her purple Grape, and gently creeps
> Luxuriant; meanwhile murmuring waters fall
> Down the slope hills, disperst, or in a Lake,
> That to the fringed Bank with Myrtle crown'd,
> Her crystal mirror holds, unite their streams.
>
> (*Paradise Lost,* IV, 246–63)

Also we know that when the young poet came to write a poem
about his "delicious Paradise," he prefaced it with a quotation
from *Comus:*

> Hesperus and his daughters three,
> That sing about the golden tree.
>
> (ll. 982–83)

The song of the Hesperides is preceded by an introduction in
Miltonic blank verse filled with rich names such as that of
"Zidonian Hanno," who sailing "Past Thymiaterion, in calmèd
bays" comes upon a land

That [runs] bloom-bright into the Atlantic blue,
Beneath a highland leaning down a weight
Of Cliffs, and zoned below with cedar shade,

and from the slope "[Come] voices, like the voices in a dream, / Continuous till he reached the outer sea."

But "The Hesperides," especially the song, owes more to Milton's *Comus* than merely its epigraph. As J. W. Mackail noticed, its "quality of romance and magic" is essentially the same as that found in the Prologue to *Comus* which appears in the Cambridge Manuscript. Moreover, Mackail believes that Tennyson had read the manuscript version of the Prologue and had "been profoundly influenced by the suppressed passage."[49]

Similarly, G. Robert Stange, who has written a most interesting interpretation of "The Hesperides," also sees a close relationship between the poems. The epigraph from *Comus* should remind us, he says, "that this nineteenth-century vision is to be compared with Milton's description (ll. 976–91) of the paradisiacal home of the Attendant Spirit."[50] And he believes that the "chief resemblance of [Tennyson's] poem to Milton's is in the parallel conception of the gardens as a restful abode for the privileged spirit and as a source of creativity—in Milton's case of the higher life, and in Tennyson's of the life of art."[51] Stange also links Tennyson's golden apples with "the Miltonic fruit of the knowledge of good and evil which must be denied man. Tennyson," he notes, "adds the essential fact that the golden fruit and the garden itself are to be protected from ordinary humanity."[52]

II   The young Tennyson's attitude toward Milton is readily apparent, as we have seen, from a study of his early poetry, but after the 1832 volume Tennyson's period of apprenticeship was over and so was the period of imitation. Although echoes of Milton are heard again and again in his later poetry, his verse technique and subject matter are genuinely his own. This change can readily be traced

in Tennyson's blank verse which was at first highly imitative as
the young poet attempted to experiment and gain insight into
its intricacies. There is ample evidence to show that he was a
student of all the great practitioners of both dramatic and non-
dramatic blank verse from Marlowe, Shakespeare, and Milton
to Thomson, Wordsworth, Shelley, and Keats. Of the older
poets, Shakespeare and Milton had the greatest influence on
Tennyson's blank verse, and of the younger poets, Tennyson
thought that "Shelley's blank verse was the finest since Milton."[53] But he felt that Keats's blank verse "lacked originality
in movement,"[54] and just before his death, he reiterated this:
"Keats," he said, "was not a master of blank verse. It might be
true of Wordsworth at his best. Blank verse can be the finest
mode of expression in our language."[55]

Evidently Tennyson knew rather early that blank verse would
be one of his major verse forms, and he deliberately set out to
master the difficult technique and mold it to his own requirements. Therefore, after a period of careful study, Tennyson's
blank verse gradually ceased to be derivative and developed
into a unique blank verse characteristic of its author alone.
Saintsbury noted that the blank verse of *The Lover's Tale* is a
much greater advance than *Timbuctoo* toward Tennyson's later
practice, and he pointed out the "peculiar and entirely novel
shaping of verse paragraphs,[56] and of verse-clauses and sentences within it [*The Lover's Tale*]."[57] Later he said that although Tennyson's blank verse is "a descendant and representative" of the Shakespearian and Miltonic verse, it is "in no way
a copy."[58]

Since the later poetry of Tennyson is not as direct in conveying to us his attitude toward Milton as is the early work,
his final view of Milton is best found in his many references
to him in letters and conversations. For instance, there are many
reports about Tennyson's reading of Milton's works aloud.
Once Tennyson confided to William Michael Rossetti "that he
knew no one so well-fitted as himself for reading Milton aloud;
as he had a deep chest and long-drawn breath, and could finish

the weighty periods of many lines together without a second inhalation."[59] During his visits to the London taverns—especially the Cock—in the late 1830's, Tennyson loved to enact "with grim humour Milton's 'so started up in his foul shape the fiend,' from the crouching of the toad to the explosion."[60] In 1870 Annie Thackeray recalled that she and the Ritchies dined with the Tennysons after which Tennyson gave a magnificent recitation of *Lycidas* and then followed it with an "unexpected outburst, 'I don't suppose one blessed German can appreciate the glory of the verse as I can.' " And when he heard that one of the group had not read *Paradise Lost* through, he said, "Shameless daughter of your age."[61]

Although he loved the other poems of Milton and refused to have anything to do with the *Golden Treasury* unless it included *Lycidas,* "L'Allegro," and "Il Penseroso,"[62] *Paradise Lost* was, of course, his favorite, and he enjoyed going through it or quoting portions from memory and making comments: "A good instance of onomatopoeia," he would say, or "This shows a fine dramatic feeling in Milton":

> Disfigured, more than could befall
> Spirit of happy sort; his gestures fierce
> He mark'd, and mad demeanour, then alone,
> As he supposed, all unobserved, unseen.

What an imagination the old man had!" he once exclaimed to his son, Hallam; "Milton beats everyone in the material sublime." Moreover, there are many comments which indicate his eye for mystic passages or particularly beautiful artistry. Tennyson admired the lines "From the arched roof / Pendant by subtle Magic many a row / Of Starry Lamps and blazing Cressets fed," because they were "mystical"; and this line, for instance, "And in the ascending seals / Of Heaven, the stars that usher evening rose," drew this remark: "This last line is lovely because it is full of vowels, which are all different. It is even a more beautiful line than those where the repetition of the same vowels or of the same consonants sometimes are so melodious."[63] Of course, these critical comments of appreciation and analysis could be listed in much greater detail, but since they merely re-emphasize Tennyson's comprehensive knowledge of *Paradise Lost,* one final remark from the poet's last days will suffice.

On his last birthday, Tennyson recited some of Milton's blank verse "with profound admiration," and when he finished the line "all the while / Sonorous metal blowing martial sounds," he exclaimed, "What a grand line!" Then he continued with another passage:

> Whose wanton passions in the sacred porch
> Ezekiel saw, when by the vision led
> His eye survey'd the dark idolatries
> Of alienated Judah.

"This," he observed, "is very like Virgil in its movement. If Virgil is to be translated it ought to be in this elaborate kind of blank verse."[64]

One might feel that this whole discussion has been focused on Tennyson's attitude toward Milton as an artist. But the concept of Milton as artist is the very heart of Tennyson's attitude, if not *the* attitude itself, for Milton's "meaning" in *Paradise Lost* or his religious and political ideas were seldom if ever noticed by Tennyson. Needless to say, he had considered them, but there is no reason to believe that he disagreed with them. The important fact to remember is that the attitudes of Milton and Tennyson toward fate and free will, passion and reason, and poetic fame were strikingly similar. Although free will was absolutely essential to their idea of man, Milton and Tennyson did not reject without considerable thought the possibility that the course of man and nature was purely a matter of chance. The emotional tension in *Lycidas* is due in part to the young poet's fear that a life of ostensible promise and purpose might be cut short by "the blind *Fury* with th' abhorred shears," an the tense drama of *In Memoriam* is again supported by the fact that science suggests that "the stars . . . blindly run" (section III, 1. 5) and that Time is merely "a maniac scattering dust, / And Life, a Fury slinging flame" (section L, ll. 7–8).

But both poets reaffirm their belief in free will. Raphael, in *Paradise Lost,* tells Adam and Eve that since God requires "our voluntary service," He "ordain'd thy will / By nature free, not overrul'd by Fate / Inextricable, or strict necessity." As a result, man freely serves God "because we freely love, as in our will / To love or not" (V, 524–40). And after all the doubts voiced about the fate of man in *In Memoriam,* Tennyson concluded that "Our wills are ours, to make them thine." (Prologue, 1. 16.)

But perhaps more than any other, the problem of reason versus passion is the most real and perilous problem in the poetry of Milton and Tennyson. "Be strong, live happy, and love," Raphael tells Adam and Eve,

> but first of all
> Him whom to love is to obey, and keep
> His great command; take heed lest Passion sway
> Thy Judgment to do aught, which else free Will
> Would not admit; thine and of all thy Sons
> The weal or woe in thee is plac't; beware.
>
> *(Paradise Lost,* VIII, 633–38)

But the judgment of Adam and Eve is swayed. And so, too, is the reason of Paris in Tennyson's "Oenone" despite the fact that he also is aware of the true path. "Self-reverence, self-knowledge, self-control," Pallas reminds the young shepherd,

> These three alone lead life to sovereign power,
> Yet not for power (power of herself
> Would come uncall'd for) but to live by law,
> Acting the law we live by without fear;
> And, because right is right, to follow right
> Were wisdom in the scorn of consequence.
>
> (ll. 142–48)

But passion in the form of Aphrodite clouds the reason of Paris, and he, too, falls. Nowhere, however, in Tennyson's poetry is the war between passion and reason more powerfully depicted than in the *Idylls of the King* where Arthur's splendid city built to music is broken and destroyed by bestial lusts and the failure of man to distinguish between the true and the false.

The tangled forest encroaches upon the city, and the animal subdues the human and "the darkness of that battle in the West / Where all of high and holy dies away," hangs over the world because man has lost his reason.[65]

Finally, if one turns again to the two elegies *Lycidas* and *In Memoriam* which lament the death of promising young men of great talent, it is apparent that the vitality of these poems comes from the fact that death is not so much the central theme as it is a background for the discussion of life. True, the earthly potentialities and fame of Edward King and Arthur Hallam were unfulfilled because they died suddenly on the threshold of their careers, but what is the significance of such an occurrence for the living, especially for two young poets of great genius? "What boots it with unecessant care / To tend the homely slighted Shepherd's trade, / And strictly meditate the thankless Muse?"[66] cried a puzzled Milton. "What fame is left for human deeds?" asked a doubtful Tennyson. What hope is there

> for modern rhyme
> To him who turns a musing eye
> On songs and deeds, and lives, that lie
> Foreshorten'd in the tract of time?[67]

Both poets, of course, answered the question and resolved the problem by suggesting that there is a heavenly fame as well as the earthly which, like all other earthly things, shall pass away. Consequently true fame

> ". . . is no plant that grows on mortal soil,
> Nor in the glistering foil
> Set off to th' world, nor in broad rumour lies,
> But lives and spreads aloft by those pure eyes
> And perfect witness of all judging *Jove;*
> As he pronounces lastly on each deed,
> Of so much fame in Heav'n expect thy meed."
>
> (*Lycidas,* ll. 78–84)

Ultimately fame "rests with God" and although on earth silence guards Hallam's fame or the fame of any other man who dies young, "somewhere out of human view" his work "is wrought with tumult and acclaim."[68]

Although the attitudes of Milton and Tennyson were similar in several important respects, the high quality of their blank verse most often impressed the Victorians. For instance, in his review of *In Memoriam,* Coventry Patmore wrote that "Mr. Tennyson's is not only the best, but the only blank verse, in a full sense of the term, which has been written since Milton."[69] And later, Tennyson's blank verse again suggested Milton's when John Addington Symonds read "Lucretius" while floating down the waterways of Venice: "I did the voluptuous verse of 'Lucretius' full justice," he wrote to Henry Sidgwick, "for I read it in my gondola as we glided by the Ducal Palace and beneath the bridges of St. Mark's. It is splendid in rhythm and in language, perhaps the most splendid of all Tennyson's essays in blank-verse, and the most gorgeously coloured piece of unrhymed English since Milton."[70]

Indeed, the lines from Shakespeare which Tennyson once quoted in reference to Milton could have been quoted by the Victorians with equal propriety in honor of both:

> This is an art
> Which does mend Nature, change it rather, but
> The art itself is Nature.[71]

VII ✒ Milton the Artist—
The Late Victorian View

Shakespeare himself, divine as are his gifts, has not, of the marks of the master, this one: perfect sureness of hand in his style. Alone of English poets, alone in English art, Milton has it; he is our one first-rate master in the grand style. He is as truly a master in his style as the great Greeks are, or Virgil, or Dante.

—MATTHEW ARNOLD

Tennyson's relationship to Milton was in many ways an anticipation of the late Victorian view of the poet, particularly in that he primarily focused his attention upon Milton's artistry and seemed to ignore the theological and philosophic content of the poetry. Moreover, Tennyson, like most later poets, did not share the early nineteenth-century compulsion to be merely original. Although he grew to manhood at a time when the "artificial" poet was believed inferior to the "original," natural genius, Tennyson's allegiance was always with the conscious artist. In this and in his careful, extensive study of the previous master artists, especially Milton and Virgil, he adhered to a pattern which the best late Victorian poets also followed.

Furthermore, while the interest of the early Victorians was in Milton's matter—his theology, setting, and characters, Tennyson and the late Victorians were primarily impressed with his form, style, and metrical skill. Robert Montgomery, Abraham Heraud and their fellow apocalyptics, as I have shown, attempted to imitate the superficial aspects of Milton's epical material, but Gerard Manley Hopkins, Coventry Patmore, and Robert Bridges were fascinated by the endless variations and consummate artistry found in the blank verse of Milton. To Byron and his contemporaries, *Paradise Lost* first of all meant "themes celestial" and "immortal wars which gods and angels wage" on an heroic scale, but to Francis Thompson and his fellow poets and critics, the epic was "the treasury and supreme display of metrical counterpoint" and Milton was "the most inspired artificer in poetry," the creator of a marvelous "conscious and consummate" art.[1]

In looking back over the changing attitudes toward Milton during the nineteenth century, it is easy enough to distinguish clearly along what lines the Victorian attitudes toward Milton developed and to recognize the principal shift in interest and emphasis from his matter and thought to his manner, style, and prosody. Too, we should remember that this movement from thought to art and beyond was not completed by 1900, but that the curve of the developing attitude toward Milton more properly culminated with T. S. Eliot and the rejection by critics and poets not only of Milton's thought but also of his art.[2] At the close of the Victorian period, Milton's art was held supreme, and it must have been well-nigh impossible for anyone to contemplate a time when Milton the artist would be condemned and his influence decried. But it must be recalled that John Keats's attitude toward Milton clearly anticipated this total curve of development as closely as Tennyson's attitude anticipated it in part.

During his early years as a poet, Keats felt that there were two things that he needed from Milton: his philosophy—his wisdom and insight into life—and a thorough knowledge of his style and poetic skill. In the poem "On Seeing a Lock of Milton's Hair," Keats greeted Milton as the "Chief of organic numbers! / Old Scholar of the Spheres!" and went on to say that his passionate desires for poetry would be vain "until I grow high-rife / With old philosophy, / And mad with glimpses of futurity!"[3] But Keats who responded to the art object as intensely as Wordsworth responded to the natural object soon found Milton's style and artistry of most interest, and began to complain about poetry which seemed to have a "palpable design" upon him. Keats, like later Victorian poets, wanted Milton's art, but he in time decided that he did not want to be "bullied" by Milton's philosophy. After the first *Hyperion,* however, Keats went a step further, and like Eliot and other post-Victorians, concluded that he did not want to be "bullied" by Milton's art. In the famous letter of 22 September, 1819, Keats looked forward to the late Victorian view of Walter Raleigh who thought of *Paradise Lost* as a "gigantic filamented structure" raised into the air, an "enchanted palace" created "by the most delicate skill of architecture,"[4] and he also anticipated the attitude of Eliot when he wrote: "The Paradise Lost, though so fine in itself, is a corruption of our language. It should be kept as it is—unique, a curiosity, a beautiful and grand curiosity, the most remarkable production of the world." Then he concluded his letter with these famous lines of rejection: "I have but lately stood on my guard against Milton. Life to him would be death to me. Miltonic verse cannot be written, but is the verse of art. I wish to devote myself to another verse alone." The late Victorians, as we shall see, did not find Milton's influence baneful as did Keats in his last phase, but rather testified to its beneficence. Yet to them, as to Keats, Milton's poetry was truly "the verse of art."

Naturally enough, the rather sharp change in attitude which occurred almost abruptly during the 1850's and 1860's and is attested to by a rejection of Milton's "philosophy" and a lively new interest in Milton's artistry was the result of the impact of various dynamic forces which radically affected the Victorian attitude toward many things other than just Milton. However, the two major factors which it is necessary to discuss here are the rapid decay of faith in orthodox religious tenets and practices, and the intense but less widely diffused interest in art which became apparent after the mid-century mark. The reasons for the almost catastrophic changes which occurred in the religious life of England after 1850 are well-known and were mainly due to the impact which books dealing with the historical criticism of the Bible, such as Bishop Colenso's critical examination of the Pentateuch and the Book of Joshua, had on society, and treatises concerning recent scientific discoveries which led up to Darwin's well-written, well-documented, and incomparable *Origin of Species.*

What is particularly germane is that critical examinations of the Bible and scientific developments clouded the theological atmosphere of Victorian England with doubt and uncertainty, and, as a result, it appeared difficult for any educated person aware of these events to maintain a firm belief in the authenticity of the Bible as the inspired (not to mention the literal) word of God, and faith in the age-old dogmas and revealed truths of Christianity. Some to their great consternation found it impossible to stay within the bounds of the orthodox religion, and unhappily wandered off into the folds of atheism or agnosticism. Others, happy to be rid of the burden which Calvinism had placed upon their consciences, gladly relegated religious problems to the past. Many, however, who maintained a belief in a divine Being even in the face of advances in Biblical criticism and science, tended more and more to shy away from unguarded, dogmatic statements of religious belief and careless, indecorus remarks about religious problems, simply because they were hardly so certain concerning the nature of God as earlier Christians had been.

Tennyson, as I have said, did not concern himself with Milton's religious thought, but rather focused attention upon his artistry. This, however, does not mean that he and later poets were uninterested in theology. It means simply that their lack of interest in Milton's religious ideas was due, in part, to his certainty and their perplexing uncertainty about the ways of God. Milton's confident descriptions of God and His relationship to man in *Paradise Lost* and his exposition of Christian theology in the *De Doctrina* whose bald, straight-forward Latin prose rings with assurance and conviction, contrasted sharply with the doubtful Victorian view which readily admitted that the ways of God to man were too complex to be comprehended. Tennyson believed, for instance, that the universe was governed by a divine Being but that knowledge of Him was almost impossible to come by and certainly not extensive enough to dogmatize about. The only evidence which he could muster in support of this belief is there in the lines:

> And like a man in wrath the heart
> Stood up and answer'd, "I have felt."

That was all that could and should be said, not only at the time Tennyson wrote it, but also in the uncertain religious atmosphere of the later Victorian period.

Of course Tennyson and others were willing to discuss theological problems in the carefully regulated, philosophical atmosphere of the Metaphysical Society in the company of a few well-chosen intellectuals; and he, himself, found it possible to express with great subtlety and precise qualification his obscure feelings and ambivalent thoughts about God and man in the dramatically distanced and artistically realized world of *In Memoriam*. But the person who glibly believed that he could with absolute certainty reduce God and His relationship to man to a series of dogmatic statements whether he be a seventeenth-century poet or a nineteenth-century divine, annoyed (if he did not absolutely pain) later Victorians.

As a result of this uncertainty, many like Walter Pater, felt that "the relative spirit" was the only one possible to the modern mind; and, in his review of Mrs. Humphry Ward's famous novel, *Robert Elsmere* (1888), Pater wrote: "Robert Elsmere was a type of a large class of minds which cannot be sure that the sacred story is true."[5]

Similarly, Leslie Stephen was typical of many who entirely lost their faith soon after Charles Darwin's *Origin of Species* was published in November of 1859. Not only did mid-century religious and scientific developments play havoc with the multitude of clergy and laymen who read the Bible in a fundamentalist fashion; it also shattered the beliefs of those who put their faith in the traditional metaphysical assumption that the universe was established upon orderly principles and that evidence for a God of reason who loved order and eschewed chaos could be seen everywhere in the nature of things. The real significance of the *Origin of Species* according to Noel Annan, lay "in its apparent contradiction of orthodox metaphysics. Darwin introduced the idea that *chance* begets order."[6]

Consequently, the new data in the area of Biblical criticism and the discoveries in geology and other sciences had one effect that outweighed all others: they caused men to feel that there could be no certainty in the realm of theology, and that religious truths, if there were any, were likely to change from age to age. Out of this attitude came, naturally enough, the major charge which the late Victorians lodged against Milton: he had, unfortunately, made the mistake of assuming that his theological position was the ultimate one. When Milton wrote, said Mark Pattison, he thought his subject "offered him the guarantees of reality, authenticity, and divine truth,"[7] and, as a result, he based his great epic, *Paradise Lost,* upon theological dogma and a literal reading of Genesis which were made obsolete by later developments. Hence the effectiveness of Milton's greatest work was seriously impaired, its popularity was greatly diminished, and, of course, the attitude of his Victorian readers was altered.

Nothing perhaps points up this change in attitude toward Milton and *Paradise Lost* so dramatically as does the decline of Satan's popularity. By the late nineteenth century, Milton's greatest and most celebrated character had lost his hold over the imagination of the Victorians. "Satan himself," said Raleigh, "is not what he used to be; he is doubly fallen in the esteem of his victims as well as of his Maker, and indeed

> Comes to the place where he before had sat
> Among the prime in splendour, now deposed,
> Ejected, emptied, gazed, unpitied, shunned,
> A spectacle of ruin.[8]

Furthermore, *Paradise Lost* became a great measuring stick whereby one could easily gauge the progress made since the seventeenth century. "Probably no book," wrote Walter Bagehot,

> shows the transition which our theology has made, since the middle of the seventeenth century, at once so plainly and so fully. We do not now compose long narratives to "justify the ways of God to man." The more orthodox we are, the more we shrink from it; the more we hesitate at such a task, the more we allege that we have no powers for it. Our most celebrated defences of established tenets are in the style of Butler, not in that of Milton. They do not profess to show a satisfactory explanation of human destiny; on the contrary, they hint that probably we could not understand such an explanation if it were given us; at any rate, they allow that it is not given us.[9]

Pattison was of the opinion that Milton's epic would have fared much better if he had "raised his imaginative fabric on a more permanent foundation; upon the appetites, passions, and emotions of men, their vices and virtues, their aims and ambitions, which are a far more constant quantity than any theological system."[10] Similarly, the only passage in Milton's poetry which evoked the unqualified admiration of Bagehot was the highly realistic Satanic council scene in Book Two of *Paradise Lost*. Bagehot admired it because of its aura of actuality which derived, he believed, from the fact that it was modelled upon debates in Parliament and Cromwell's council which Milton had carefully observed. The question before the council, said Bagehot, is "very practical," and "though the formal address is to devils, the real address is to men: to the human nature which we know, not to the fictitious demonic nature we do not know."[11]

As to Milton's untroubled certainty about his theological views and the scheme of things, it was attributed by most Victorians to his Puritanism and what they felt to be its necessary concomitant, a rigid belief that the Bible story was literally true. For instance, Mark Pattison was of the opinion that the poet never questioned the idea that the Old Testament was a revelation from God. "Nor did he," Pattison continued, "only receive these books as conveying in substance a divine view of the world's history, he regarded them as in the letter a transcript of fact."[12] That Milton read the Bible literally rather than figuratively is, of course, not quite true, but Pattison's view was almost universally accepted by late Victorians. John Ruskin was among the very few who dared to say that Milton's account of the fall of the angels was "evidently unbelievable to himself,"[13] and he was specifically rebuked by Pattison, Garnett, and others for saying so. "Milton undoubtedly believed most fully in the actual existence of all his chief personages, natural and supernatural," wrote Richard Garnett, "and was sure that, however he might have indulged his imagination in the invention of incidents, he had represented character with the fidelity of a conscientious historian."[14]

Since this was the Victorian consensus of opinion, the fortunes of *Paradise Lost* were bound to be tied up closely with the book of Genesis. Once people came to believe that the Old Testament descriptions of the Creation, the Flood, and the Ten Commandments were mere myths and had neither divine inspiration nor scientific fact to back them up, all the reverence, awe, and respect belonging to a sacred book of absolute literal truth rapidly fell away. Since *Paradise Lost* was based solidly upon the early chapters of Genesis, it merited reverence and maintained the authority of a sacred book only so long as Genesis commanded the respect of the faithful. Once Genesis lost its special position as a sacred oracle, *Paradise Lost* suffered a similar fate. If, therefore the subject matter and thought content of Milton's epic were to maintain their vitality and hold over the minds of the Victorians, it must either come to be read as myth like Homer's epics, or it must be read as a figurative representation of divine truths. Since some Victorians were strangely unable to see the plausibility of reading Genesis figuratively rather than literally, they likewise tended to resist any effort to read *Paradise Lost* in this light. Matthew Arnold is a notable example of those who believed that the epic had to be discarded if it could not be read and believed to be a literal description of things as they really were. *Paradise Lost,* said Arnold, is not so much a theological poem as a commentary on the first two or three chapters of Genesis: "Its subject, therefore, is a story, taken literally, which many of even the most religious people nowadays hesitate to take literally." The whole real interest of the epic, he stoutly maintained, depends upon the ability of the reader to take it literally. "Merely as a matter of poetry, the story of the Fall has no special force or effectiveness; its effectiveness for us comes, and can only come, from our taking it all as the literal narrative of what positively happened."[15]

This attitude, of course, was soundly refuted by Augustine Birrell. But he defended the epic not upon the possibility of a figurative interpretation; rather, like Coleridge, he based his view upon the idea that the fable and characters of *Paradise Lost* were not derived from the Bible but merely suggested by it. "The poem," he said,

> proceeds upon a legend, ancient and fascinating, and to call it a commentary on Genesis is a marvellous criticism. The Story of the Fall of Man, as recorded in the Semitic legend, is to me more attractive as a story than the Tale of Troy, and I find the rebellion of Satan and his dire revenge more to my mind than the circles of Dante. Eve is, I think, more interesting than "Heaven-born Helen, Sparta's queen,"—I mean in herself, and as a woman to write poetry about.[16]

Just why so many Victorians thought that Milton believed the Genesis story to be literally true when there are ample indications in *Paradise Lost* and the *De Doctrina* to demonstrate that Milton perhaps thought otherwise, is not clear;[17] but it should be remembered that the earlier nineteenth century was just as addicted to a literal reading of the Scriptures as was the seventeenth century. The figurative interpretation of the Bible, old as the Church fathers, was certainly not unfamiliar to Milton and many of his contemporaries. But with the Reformation had come the emphasis on the Bible as *the* authority in theological matters, and in Milton's own day as was indicated in an earlier chapter, the Puritans believed that the New Testament literally spelled out the correct form of Church government. By the nineteenth century, views such as these which encouraged a literal reading of the Bible had had a cumulative effect. As a result, among dissenters and Evangelicals, the tradition of literalism was strongly and unquestioningly entrenched. Consequently, late nineteenth-century critics generally assumed that most Englishmen up to their day were literalists in their interpretation of the Bible. Milton, like most Puritans, critics assumed, believed that every word of Genesis was fact:

> For Milton and the men of his time, the first chapters of Genesis were as literally true as any facts of English history. In all the spiritual existences of the "Paradise Lost," not only in the angels and demons, but even in the heathen gods as evil spirits, Milton and his contemporaries had as implicit faith as they had in the existence of Moses and Aaron. But this, which enhanced the power of his subject for that age, has somewhat impaired its hold on ours. Few men now conceive of the unseen world exactly as Milton did. His entire theology, his dialogues between the Father and the Son, and his whole celestial atmosphere, are, even at the best, frigid.[18]

If the Victorian critics had realized that Milton did not necessarily believe that the Old Testament stories were literally true, their peevishness toward what they conceived to be Milton's outdated, narrow theological concepts would have been lessened. But the fact remains that Milton did very definitely believe the Bible was divinely inspired, and since many late Victorians believed neither that the Bible was literally true nor divinely inspired, their attitude toward Milton's theology would not have been seriously modified. In the light of Raphael's intriguing question,

> . . . though what if Earth
> Be but the shadow of Heav'n, and things therein
> Each to other like, *more than on Earth is thought?*
>
> (*Paradise Lost,* V, 574–76)

perhaps Keightley was closer to the truth than most of his contemporaries when with caution he wrote that "it is highly probable that he [Milton] believed the creations of his imagination to be almost identical with the actual condition of the universe, and that he was describing the real Heaven, Hell, and Chaos."[19]

However that may be, Milton was, time and time again, indicted for confidently believing "that the plain and brief story which he drew from the Bible would never lose credit." Milton, wrote H. Rawlings in his article, "The Transfigured Theology of 'Paradise Lost,'" "was filled with the magnificent hope of handing down to posterity, in a new and glorifying dress, truths of eternal significance and of universal interest. Two hundred years, and especially the last fifty years, have brought Milton's posterity to a different point of view. What he supposed to be a divine revelation turns out to be human invention. What he regarded as solemn truth we regard as fanciful myth."[20]

But after once again rephrasing and restating the usual indictment, Rawlings, like most of his contemporaries, had to come face to face with the really important question for the late Victorians: "Is this mighty epic [*Paradise Lost*], hitherto regarded as one of the great masterpieces of English literature and one of the sublimest productions of human genius, henceforth valueless for those who do not accept its Biblical and theological basis?"[21] In attempting to give an answer, Rawlings noticed that "many liberal thinkers" had already answered the question by persistently neglecting *Paradise Lost*. But Rawlings believed that the epic had not lost its value and still had a place in the modern world. However, he was careful to point out that the status of *Paradise Lost* had changed, and that it could never occupy the same place in the minds and hearts of Englishmen which it once held "when men put it beside the Bible and regarded it almost as a new scripture of the true faith."[22]

Instead of attempting to revive interest in *Paradise Lost* on the basis of its past glory, Rawlings attempted to look ahead to the time when the anti-theological feeling which it provoked in his day would be impossible simply because "its theology will be dead, and there will be nothing to disturb the full enjoyment of its plot, its splendid imaginative pictures, the majestic roll of its verse, its abounding pearls of beautiful speech and noble wisdom."[23] Rawlings and many eminent Victorians believed that in order to preserve Milton's reputation, Milton the didactic theologian had to be forgotten, and Milton the artist had to be brought to the fore.

Rawlings, however, was aware of one fact which the Victorian *avant-garde* often appeared to overlook. Although modern thought had given the theology of *Paradise Lost* its "mortal wound," Rawlings saw clearly that it was "a long time dying": the epic's theology "is still able to marshal strong social forces and the power of majorities against those who dare to impugn it." Therefore, the critic declared, the theology at this moment when old and new thoughts are struggling together cannot be ignored. In fact, it was Rawlings' purpose to show that if the theology of *Paradise Lost* is studied, one will find that Milton inadvertently and unconsciously demonstrated the falseness and absurdity of the epic's theology. "The most obvious and yet the most telling criticisms upon the Bible story of the Fall, when interpreted in the traditional way, are these—that the whole account is miserably meagre for so stupendous an event; and that the *causes* of the catastrophe and the way in which it took place are altogether trivial and unintelligible."[24]

It is Rawlings' most important point that Milton himself unconsciously realized this; he subconsciously knew that the Genesis story was not adequate to explain rationally or justify sufficiently the ways of God to man. Because Milton was primarily a poet, and only secondarily a theologian, he was able with the promptings of his subconscious desires to transform the inadequate notions of his scriptural theology into a more adequate exposition of the human condition. Therefore, since Milton did not believe the account in Genesis of the Fall, he

placed the fundamental ideas of the traditional Christian system in an "unfavourable light" without actually knowing it.
"Now in *Paradise Lost,*" he continued, "the theme [of the Fall]
is at least treated with fulness and dignity. The length of the
poem is worthy of the issues. The crisis is elaborately led up to.
There is a serious attempt to make the causes clear and show
them to be sufficient. Bravely is the question of divine justice
wrestled with." Thus, "all the new resources which he employs
in aid of his attempt are themselves so many unconscious criticisms upon the Bible story."[25]

In short, as Rawlings saw it, Milton, in *Paradise Lost* was
exploring and attempting to find answers, in human terms, to
the perplexing problems of human destiny. Milton, while consciously thinking he could answer all these questions within
the framework of his puritan theological doctrine, unconsciously
failed to accept these explanations as adequate and fully satisfying; therefore, he unconsciously went *beyond* the meagre
scriptural data and elaborated upon it, and pushed into theo-
logically unauthorized realms in his attempt to arrive at a more
rationally and imaginatively satisfying explanation of man and
the universe. Consequently, said Rawlings, "Milton has ruined
the Genesis fable for theology. But this result is from our modern
point of view no calamity, but the contrary. The recognition of
it is even the essential condition of an intelligent appreciation
of the splendid poetic structure for which Milton used the
Biblical fragments."[26]

Since Milton had demonstrated in his handling of *Paradise
Lost* that the orthodox theology was not believable, he did, so
to speak, free the modern reader from any need to think it so.
According to Rawlings, the late Victorian was at liberty to
recognize *Paradise Lost* for what it really was, a splendid work
of poetic artistry. Those who "have given up the old theology,"
Rawlings assured his readers, need no longer neglect *Paradise
Lost,* because they are no longer under any obligation to feel
that they are expected to believe its main story as a truth of
religion. Rawlings' final conclusion was that in "this age of

science and Biblical criticism," *Paradise Lost* must be read "as a poem and not as a theology. Only when you feel yourself absolutely free to doubt any of its episodes as history, can you properly enjoy them as poetry, as the creation of man's thought and imagination."[27]

In Rawlings' essay, we can see how late nineteenth-century developments in science and religion led to a complete rejection of Milton's theology and turned the readers' attention toward his artistry—the "majestic roll" of his verse; his "abounding pearls of beautiful speech." Modes of looking at science, theology, and art, characteristic of the late Victorian period, had commingled, modified, and complemented each other in the erratic way typical of movements in thought, to form the late nineteenth-century attitude toward Milton, an attitude which was quite different from the early Victorian view.[28]

Milton, who was, it seems to me, a rather popular poet during the first half of the century, became a relatively unread author during the latter half-century. This decline was, of course, primarily the result of shifts in religious sentiment and movements in art, but, in addition, I think we must agree with Edward Dowden that the publication of the *De Doctrina* in 1825 had initiated a relatively silent but certain change in sentiment on the part of many devout people, and that in many homes *Paradise Lost* "could no longer be considered a safe soporific for Sunday afternoons."[29] Furthermore, as the Chartist Movement and the "hungry forties" became a memory, and republican agitation—which was largely responsible for drawing attention to Milton's prose works—subsided, Milton's popular reading public declined rapidly.

Certainly Milton, the writer of apocalyptic religious epics, the sensationally sublime poet who captivated the imagination of the early, more romantic Victorians, was more appealing and more easily comprehended by a popular audience than the Milton who was valued by a more sophisticated late Victorian audience for his style and subtle metrical achievements—the

kind of group, for instance, which Robert Bridges referred to
when he said that Tennyson educated an audience which was
"specially observant of blemishes, and who came to regard
finish not only as indispensable, but as the one satisfying
positive quality."[30]

Milton, therefore, during the later years of the century was
the object of the enthusiasm of a rather small, select group of
poets and critics who like Landor, Tennyson, Arnold, and Walter Raleigh valued him for his consummate artistry. But even
the late Victorian show of unanimity concerning Milton's art
was, beneath the surface, a bit more complicated than is generally assumed. It is too often taken for granted that Raleigh's
attitude toward Milton's artistry is the typical one, and, of
course, to a certain extent it is. But it seems to me that Raleigh's
view was entirely too feeble to be representative of those poets
like Hopkins and Bridges who had a much more vital, more
worthy conception of Milton's art.

Sir Walter Raleigh's biography of Milton is often thought
to be the classic statement of *the* late nineteenth-century view
of Milton's art, when, in fact, it should be looked upon as the
classic statement of a group of critics and poets who like Keats
thought of Milton's art as a unique, fragile curiosity—"a
beautiful and grand curiosity."[31] Certainly Raleigh's work is a
brilliant example of those criticisms of *Paradise Lost* which picture it as a "gigantic filamented structure," a delicate dream-
like *objet d'art* which stands precariously on the sheer cliff of
Milton's marvelous genius—an unbelievable *tour de force* never
again to be duplicated.

Fortunately, however, there were poets during the century
who saw great strength where Raleigh tended to see only pre-
ciosity; there were those who, unlike Raleigh, believed that
Milton's soundness of touch and brilliant metrical achievements
could and should be duplicated and emulated. These poets never
thought of *Paradise Lost* as a kind of hot-house plant which
was to be put upon a pedestal and "admired" from a distance.
Rather they *used* as well as admired its art; they profited by

a close study of its strong, sure structure and metrical patterns. Although Tennyson, Arnold, Bridges, and others tended to agree with Raleigh that *Paradise Lost* was "a monument to dead ideas," a sculptured piece like Michelangelo's which was to be admired for its form, style, and superb artistry,[32] they went far beyond his dubiously appreciative, admiring attitude to an *active participation* in the strength and magnificence of Milton's art.

These practicing poets, whose attitude toward Milton cannot be represented by Raleigh's, had, as I shall show, some important things in common. Besides a genuine devotion to Milton, Victorians like Landor, Tennyson, Arnold, Patmore, Hopkins, and Bridges shared, first of all, an interest in the literature of ancient Greece and Rome; second, an unusual preoccupation with the artistic aspects of poetry—its style and prosody; and, third, a deep commitment to a conscious artistry founded upon a thorough, intimate knowledge of the great artistic poets of the past.

That Milton's most ardent followers were to a large extent also "classicists" should be particularly noticed, because it is also true that another well-known group of poets, the Pre-Raphaelites, devoted medievalists, were noticeably cold, even hostile, toward Milton. Since Milton, the artist, was the subject of considerable attention during the "arty" eighties and "yellow" nineties, it should not be assumed that all the poets devoted to art were therefore also dedicated students of Milton's art. For although Dante Gabriel Rossetti and especially William Morris, "the idle singer of an empty day," came closer to an art for art's sake position than poets such as Hopkins and Bridges, it did not bring them closer to Milton. To be sure, the poets who found Milton's work an inspiration did share with the Pre-Raphaelites the late Victorian interest in art, the pseudo-scientific mania for precise detail, and, in particular, a firm belief in conscious artistry. But the two groups did not share a common devotion to Milton for several reasons. First, the Pre-Raphaelites were far less interested in politics, religion, and contemporary events than were the classicists; in fact, Milton's religious sentiments and political preoccupations were so distasteful to Rossetti and the early Morris that they proved to be an insuperable barrier to any potential interest in his art. Moreover, the Pre-Raphaelites' dislike of classicism and their devout interests in medievalism were obstacles in their path toward understanding a poet whose work is practically devoid of anything remotely resembling the spirit and chief characteristics of the Middle Ages.[33]

It is, then, to be remembered that the critics and poets who sang Milton's praises during the late nineteenth century were those who also had a strong tie with the literature of Greece and Rome and were only rarely and incidentally interested in medievalism. Hopkins, for instance, is a signal example of this since, despite his Catholicism, he found no interest in what W. H. Gardner calls Morris' "artificial Romantic medievalism," but rather considered himself a part of a classical tradition in English literature which extended from Milton through Gray, Landor, and Arnold up to Robert Bridges.[34]

Tennyson, as we have seen, anticipated Hopkins and Bridges in his simultaneous devotion to both the ancient Greek and Roman poets and Milton. But he was not alone in this. Walter Savage Landor and Matthew Arnold, as well as Swinburne to some extent, exhibit the same devotion. For example, Landor's whole life as an artist was bound up in Greek and Latin literature, but his devotion to Milton's art was equally strong. Early in his poetic career, Landor, who thought of poetry as an "elegant accomplishment," came to the conclusion that Milton, alone among the moderns, possessed invention, energy, and grandeur of design, the "three great requisites to constitute a great poet."[35] Accordingly, he apprenticed himself to a study of Milton's art. Devoted as he was to classical literature, Landor admitted that his prejudices in its favor "began to wear away on *Paradise Lost;* and even the great hexameter sounded to me tinkling, when I had recited in my solitary walks on the seashore the haughty appeal of Satan and the deep penitence of

Eve."[36] Landor's best early work, the epic poem *Gebir,* composed about 1797, reflects in its blank verse and diction his close study of *Paradise Lost.*[37]

The poetry of Matthew Arnold, likewise reflects the attention the young poet gave to Milton's work. Arnold freely admitted that in *Sohrab and Rustum* he attempted to emulate Milton's grandeur as well as his classic restraint and objectivity,[38] and Lionell Trilling has said that "the model Arnold had in mind for his free forms was Milton in the choruses of *Samson Agonistes.*"[39] Certainly no one was more aware of Milton's kinship to the classical authors than Arnold who in his Milton Address declared: "If this host of readers [those who knew no Greek] are ever to gain any sense of the power and charm of the great poets of antiquity, their way to gain it is not through translations of the ancients, but through the original poetry of Milton, who has the like power and charm, because he has the like great style."[40] This particular ingredient in Milton's art was, of course, *the* element which consciously or unconsciously appealed to those poets from Landor and Tennyson to Hopkins and Bridges who recognized in Milton the same kinship to classicism which they desired. Since Milton was able to transfuse English poetry with the power, charm, and great style of the ancient poets, he naturally was more useful and exerted a greater influence on these poets than did the ancients themselves.

The second and third factors which Milton's followers shared were a devotion to art, especially its technical aspects, and a firm commitment to conscious artistry. In the chapter on Shakespeare and Milton I showed that Milton was invariably downgraded, so to speak, because he was a conscious artist whose work appeared to early nineteenth-century critics to have an aura of artificiality about it. On the other hand, Shakespeare was in the eyes of many romantics a "natural" intuitive poet whose plays were the very essence of "unpremeditated art." But by the late decades of the Victorian period, this ideal of the untutored poet whose poetry was in no way derived from the literature of the past, was replaced by an opposite, largely "un-romantic" ideal, that of the skilled, conscious artist who like Virgil endeavored to polish and perfect each verse.

Laurence Binyon once wrote that in England, "poetry is not commonly thought of as an art but rather as a sort of spontaneous ebullition of emotion, with something of an implicit antithesis between art and inspiration."[41] The poets whom we are considering made a definite attempt to change this attitude toward poetry, for the way in which they conceived of the poet as conscious artist was in keeping with a nineteenth-century tendency to think of the "artist" not as just any skilled laborer, but as a person *skilled* in the creative or imaginative arts.[42] More and more the poets, following the lead of the painters, liked to think of themselves as *skilled craftsmen* who despite natural talent must spend years in painful, dedicated study of the great craftsmen of the past. Less and less was said about the primitive, uncultivated artist who warbled woodnotes wild. Training and discipline which included an intimate knowledge of poetic progress came to be recognized as the true way to great artistry.

Conventry Patmore voiced the late Victorian attitude when he wrote that

> the lives and the works of all great artists, poets or otherwise, show that the free spirit of art has been obtained, not by neglect, but by perfection of discipline. Dante, Shakespeare, Milton and Goethe, perhaps the highest poetical names of the Christian era, prove clearly enough to any one truly acquainted with their spirit, that the laws of art, as far as those were known at their respective periods, had been studied by them as matters of science, and that it was by working on the platform of such knowledge that they achieved strains of poetry which exceeded the laws and limits of all previous art.

No poet can ever be truly great and originate laws of his own, Patmore declared, "unless he himself has learned to comprehend those which are the legacy of his predecessors."[43]

Since conscious artistry also entailed the close study and emulation of earlier poets, the late Victorian poets had no misgivings about imitating Milton's poetry. Unlike Keats and Eliot, they never found the art of Milton a bad influence nor a threat to their own originality. Like Pope and any other poet who considered himself a part of a great tradition, Patmore, Hopkins, and Bridges knew how "to imitate without loss of originality, how to make use of the resources of other poets and other poetic modes" and yet remain themselves and the same.[44] For instance, what Frederick Pollock said in reference to Tennyson, could be applied with equal force to his later contemporary poets: "Lord Tennyson, far too exquisite an artist to be ever a mere imitator, has in his perfection of form been a true follower of Milton's spirit."[45] Like Bridges, these poets studied Milton "as a painter or composer studies an earlier master," analyzing and mastering his "technical experiments and valuable innovations; trying, above all, to understand the emotions and mental attitudes which their styles conveyed."[46]

In addition to their praise of his conscious artistry, the late Victorians applauded Milton's "scientific" skill in metrics. "In the *science* of his art Milton stands alone among the English poets, without equal or second," said J. W. Mackail. "It is this beyond all else which makes him, in the full sense of the word, a classic."[47] As a result, the prosody-conscious poets of the late nineteenth century who paid close attention to the blank verse of Milton, Hopkins, and Bridges, in particular, were fascinated by the choruses of *Samson Agonistes*. Soon not only the poets but the critics as well came to believe with John Addington Symonds that "to the lover of the most exalted poetry, *Samson Agonistes,* even as regards its versification, may even offer a pleasure more subtle and more rare than *Paradise Lost.*"[48]

The late Victorian study of Milton's prosody led to a new and more accurate appreciation of *Samson Agonistes,* but it also convinced the Victorians that Milton's metrical art had never been truly understood, nor had its uniqueness and brilliance been fully recognized. In a letter to his mother dated 1 March 1877, Gerard Manley Hopkins sent her two sonnets with "a few metrical effects, mostly after Milton" and noticed that "these rhythms are not commonly understood."[49] Bridges who believed that Hopkins was the first person to fully appreciate Milton's metrical intentions in the choruses of *Samson,* said in *Milton's Prosody* that "Milton's main purpose in his later writing was to invent an English prosody which should be independent of rhyme, ~~that is, using rhyme only as an ornament~~: and he shows in the choruses of *Samson* how the metric prosodial fiction of *Paradise Lost* allow the disyllabic verse to take on a great variety of free rhythms—and this metric system has never been understood by his critics."[50]

The attitude of Hopkins and Bridges who defended the irregularities in Milton's blank verse and his daring departures from strict rules was supported by other critics as well. Symonds, for example, maintained that during the Restoration and eighteenth century, "what was essentially national in our poetry —the music of sustained periods, elastic in their structure, and governed by the subtlest laws of melody in recurring consonants and vowels—was sacrificed for the artificial elegance and monotonous cadence of the couplet."[51] In a discussion of Dr. Johnson's essay on Milton's versification, Symonds stated that the treatise proved "the want of intelligence which prevailed in the last century [concerning Milton's prosody], and shows to what extent the exclusive practice of the couplet had spoiled the ear of critics for all the deeper and more subtle strains of which our language is capable." Dr. Johnson, he went on to say, "attempted to reduce blank verse to rule by setting up the standard of the ideal line, any deviation from which was to be called 'licentious, impure, unharmonious,' remaining ignorant the while that the whole effect of this metre depends upon the massing of lines in periods and on the variety of complicated cadences." It is the deviation from an ideal, he emphasized, "that constitutes the beauty of blank verse."[52]

Conventry Patmore, in his essay on the "English Metrical Critics," supported the same position, that calculated irregularity was the essence of great verse: "The over-smooth and

'accurate' metre of much of the eighteenth century poetry, to
an ear able to appreciate the music of Milton and the best
parts of Coleridge, is almost as great a defect as the entire
dissolution of metre displayed by most of the versifiers of our
own time."[53] Patmore went on to admonish his readers who believed that "smoothness" is the highest praise of versification,
when it is, in fact, "about the lowest and most easily attainable
of all its qualities. . . . In the greatest work of the greatest
metrist who ever lived, Milton, there is," he concluded, "no
long and elaborate strain of verse without one or more lines
which, though probably the most effective in the passage, will
seem to be scarcely verse at all when taken out of it."[54] Long
before T. S. Eliot, these men knew that Milton was, outside the
theatre, "the greatest master in our language of freedom within
form."[55]

This fascination with the intricate irregularities in Milton's
verse was, no doubt, partly due to the idea that the prosody of
Milton and in particular the metrics of *Samson* approximated
the brilliantly manipulated rhythms of the great Greek metrists.
For instance, Gerard Manley Hopkins, according to Gardner,
"regarded the calculated irregularities of Milton's verse as the
first significant attempt to achieve the rhythmic felicity of Greek
and Latin verse."[56] In addition, this idea was complemented by
a feeling that it took much more skill, artistic effort, and genius
to compose the choruses of *Samson Agonistes* than it took to
write the verse of "The Vanity of Human Wishes."

Conventry Patmore, like Hopkins and Bridges, was obsessed
by the intricacies of prosody; once Alice Meynell said that
when Patmore talked of his poems, "it was of their metres."[57]
Naturally he was impressed by Milton's prosody, and long before he became a poet, Patmore found Milton's poems important
to him. In his somewhat fanciful book, *Chatworth,* Patmore's
father wrote that his son's "sole idol in the temple of poetry"
was Milton. The young Patmore is pictured by the father as a
carefree, imaginative boy who was either "lapped in the Elysium
of his [Milton's] divine music, or lost in the mazes of its mar-

vellous imagery, or transfixed by the flaming sword of its majestic eloquence."[58] Patmore, whose later poetry became more and more Miltonic, was especially interested in Milton's "Nativity Ode" and the introductory verses of "L'Allegro" and "Il Penseroso" which he often cited as examples of his own idea of what the ode should be. When he wrote the odes in *The Unknown Eros,* he no doubt had Wordsworth's "Immortality Ode" and these early poems in mind.[59]

But the two late Victorian poets who profited most from their study of Milton were Gerard Manley Hopkins and Robert Bridges. These men who liked to think of themselves as poets in the classical tradition both recognized Milton as their master. Hopkins, who felt that no critic had done full justice to Milton's art, once thought of writing a treatise on Milton's metrical and lyrical art. Although I have discussed Hopkins' study of Milton's sonnets in an earlier chapter, and although Hopkins' letters and notebooks are full of references and remarks about Milton, one most important letter, that of 5 October 1878, addressed to R. W. Dixon, must be quoted extensively here, because it conveys to us in Hopkins' own words his essential attitude toward Milton.

> Milton's art is incomparable, not only in English literature but, I should think, almost in any; equal, if not more than equal, to the finest of Greek and Roman. And considering that this is shewn especially in his verse, his rhythm and metrical system, it is amazing that so great a writer as Newman should have fallen into the blunder of comparing the first chorus of *Agonistes* with the opening of [Southey's] *Thalaba* as instancing the gain in smoothness and correctness of versification made since Milton's time—Milton having been not only ahead of his own time as well as all aftertimes in verse-structure but these particular choruses being his own highwater mark. It is as if you were to compare the Panathenaic frieze and a teaboard and decide in the teaboard's favour.
>
> I have paid a good deal of attention to Milton's versification and collected his later rhythms. . . . I found his most advanced effects in the *Paradise Regained* and, lyrically, in the *Agonistes*.

Hopkins went on to speak of his experiments with poems in

what he termed "sprung rhythm" and "counterpoint," and then said: "I should add that Milton is the great standard in the use of counterpoint. In *Paradise Lost* and *Regained,* in the last more freely, it being an advance in his art, he employs counterpoint more or less everywhere, markedly now and then; but the choruses of *Samson Agonistes* are in my judgment counterpointed throughout; that is, each line (or nearly so) has two differing coexisting scansions."[60] In Dixon's reply of 10 January 1879, he wrote: "I say with you that Milton is the central man of the world for style: not only of England, but of all the world, ancient and modern."[61]

Robert Bridges, like Dixon, also was impressed by the important place that Milton occupied in our literature, and, in a review of Mackail's *The Springs of Helicon,* he cautioned his readers not to forget "how Milton connects Shakespeare with Keats, how he finally moderniz'd and methodiz'd Chaucer's metrical inventions; how he has been the strongest and most enduring of all influences on the subsequent progress of English poetry."[62] Bridges, of course, was an important defender of Milton throughout his long life, and no study of Milton and the late Victorians would be complete without a recognition of Bridges' relationship to Milton. Albert J. Guerard, in his study of Bridges, writes that "there is perhaps a closer affinity between the artistic aims of Milton and Bridges than between those of any other English poets. Both regarded lyric poetry as an art rather than as a vehicle for the expression of personality, and both were consequently stylists in the best sense." Furthermore, Guerard notices how the "same individualism and imaginative autonomy combines in both poets with a traditionalism seeking its inspiration in very diverse and apparently irreconcilable sources. Both knew classical literature, and wrote poems in Latin. . . . Unlike Keats, Bridges never tried to escape Miltonic influence, for he knew Milton to be at the very center of English poetry."[63]

Bridges, it must be remembered, was from the beginning primarily concerned with the art of poetry. He tells us that he regarded poetry from the "artistic side," not the emotional. "What led me to poetry was the inexhaustible satisfaction of form, the magic of speech, lying as it seemed to me in the masterly control of the material."[64] The "artistic side" of Milton, and especially what he called Milton's "style of execution" captivated him.[65]

More traditional and less interested in extravagant or startling departures from classical standards in verse, Bridges was closer to Milton, Arnold, and Landor than to Browning. And just as his sonnets were consciously modelled on Milton's, so was his blank verse. For example, Bridges' earliest dramatic work, *Prometheus the Firegiver,* which appeared in 1884, is in the tradition of *Samson Agonistes,* Arnold's *Merope,* and Swinburne's *Erechtheus,* but, in the opinion of J. W. Mackail, Bridges' *Prometheus* "comes nearer, perhaps, to the Greek spirit and tone than any English play that has been written since Milton." Combining Bridges' two great loves in his first important work, the Greek spirit and Milton's "style of execution," the three choruses display a remarkable technical skill. The last chorus, beginning,

> O miserable man, hear now the worst.
> O weak and tearful race,
> Born to unhappiness, see now thy cause
> Doomed and accurst![66]

is written in irregular and partially rhymed iambic verse very reminiscent of the choruses of *Samson Agonistes.* Although the drama was modeled primarily after *Samson,* it bears, in places, a striking resemblance to Milton's *Comus.* Its opening lines, which Guerard says are "the first perfect imitation of Miltonic blank verse in two hundred years of experiment" are clearly derived from the opening lines of Milton's masque:

> From high Olympus and the aetherial courts,
> Where Zeus our angry King confirms
> The Fates' decrees and bends the wills of the gods,
> I come: and on the earth step with glad foot. . . .[67]

However, the early direct imitations of Milton's poetry found alike in the poetry of Bridges or his contemporaries such as Hopkins, Arnold, Tennyson, and Landor are of little importance other than that they amply illustrate the early devotion which these poets had for Milton. A fact of more significance is that some of the great Victorian poets found Milton's art to be an important source of inspiration; it was the example of his work which spurred them on to great art.

Although modern poets have not, like Bridges and his contemporaries, looked to Milton's poetry for guidance and inspiration, our modern attitudes toward the poet have developed from certain late nineteenth-century critical viewpoints. For instance, by focusing their attention on the artificiality and "fragility" of his art, critics such as Sir Walter Raleigh created the impression that Milton was an unreliable guide and model for poets, especially those who later sought a more natural, colloquial poetic idiom. In addition, late Victorian critics and poets prepared the way for the important Christian Humanist view of Milton by attempting to stress Milton's classical rather than his Puritan orientation. Finally—and perhaps most important—the late Victorians who were no longer able to relate Milton's thought to their own post-Darwinian position lapsed into the situation in which we find ourselves today; that is, an intimate relationship no longer existed between Milton and the society of late nineteenth-century England. This more impersonal, less subjective situation paved the way for a more objective view and made it possible for recent critics, free from religious and political prejudice, to address themselves to the question of what Milton really "meant." Perhaps by this approach, by objectively ascertaining the actual intent of Milton's work and the true bent of his intellectul temper, modern critics can in time re-establish, at least on a limited scale, Milton's relevance to a large and complex society.

Reference Matter

☞ Notes

The following short titles are used throughout the notes:

Carlyle, *Works*   Thomas Carlyle, *The Works of Thomas Carlyle.* 30 vols. London: Chapman and Hall, 1899 (Centenary edition).

Coleridge, *Works*   Samuel Taylor Coleridge, *The Complete Works of Samuel Taylor Coleridge.* Edited by W. G. T. Shedd. 7 vols. New York: Harper and Brothers, 1884.

Hazlitt, *Works*   William Hazlitt, *The Complete Works of William Hazlitt.* Edited by P. P. Howe. 21 vols. London and Toronto: J. M. Dent, 1931.

Landor, *Works*   Walter Savage Landor, *The Complete Works of Walter Savage Landor.* Edited by T. Earle Welby. 16 vols. London: Chapman and Hall, 1927–36.

Macaulay, *Essays*   Thomas B. Macaulay, *Critical and Historical Essays.* 2 vols. New York: E. P. Dutton, 1907 (Everyman's Library edition).

Masson, *Essays*   David Masson, *Essays Biographical and Critical: Chiefly on English Poets.* Cambridge: Macmillan, 1856.

Minor Poems   John Milton, *Paradise Regained, the Minor Poems, and Samson Agonistes.* Edited by Merritt Y. Hughes. New York: Odyssey Press, 1937.

Ruskin, *Works*   John Ruskin, *The Works of John Ruskin.* Edited by E. T. Cook and Alexander Wedderburn. 39 vols. London: George Allen, 1903–12 (Library edition).

Schiller, *Works*   Johann Christoph Friedrich von Schiller, *Works of Friedrich Schiller.* 8 vols. Boston: S. E. Cassino, 1884.

Shelley, *Works*   Percy Bysshe Shelley, *The Works of Percy Bysshe Shelley in Verse and Prose.* Edited by Harry Buxton Forman. 8 vols. London: Reeves and Turner, 1880.

Tennyson, *Works*   Alfred Tennyson, *The Complete Poetical Works of Tennyson.* Boston: Houghton Mifflin, 1898 (Cambridge edition).

Full bibliographical information for other works not included in the Bibliography is given at the first mention of those titles in each chapter.

I. A POWER AMONGST POWERS

1   Thomas De Quincey, "On Milton," in *The Collected Writings of Thomas De Quincey,* ed. David Masson (14 vols., Edinburgh, 1890), X, 399.

2   Alfred Tennyson, "Milton" (Alcaics), in *Works,* p. 268.

3   Matthew Arnold, "Milton," in *Essays in Criticism, Second Series* (London, 1898), p. 63.

4   Thomas Macaulay, "Milton," in *Essays,* I, 158.

5   Thomas Keightley, *An Account of the Life, Opinions, and Writings of John Milton with an Introduction to Paradise Lost* (London, 1853), pp. v–vi.

6   Augustine Birrell, "John Milton," in *Obiter Dicta, Second Series* (New York, 1894), p. 44.

7   Elizabeth Barrett Browning, *The Letters of Robert Browning and Elizabeth Barrett Browning, 1845–46* (2 vols., New York, 1899), II, 261–62.

8   See John Ashton, *Eighteenth Century Waifs* (London, 1887), pp. 55–82.

9   *Ibid.,* p. 56.

10   John Keats, "On Seeing a Lock of Milton's Hair," in *The Complete Poetical Works of Keats* (Boston, 1899), pp. 39–40. For Keats's description of the incident, see in the same edition Letter #30 to Benjamin Bailey, January 23, 1818, pp. 283–84.

11   "Milton's Rib-bone," *Notes and Queries* (First Series), V (April 17, 1852), 369.

12   R. K. Webb, "The Victorian Reading Public," *Universities Quarterly,* XII (November, 1957), 25.

13 Thomas Cooper, *The Life of Thomas Cooper Written by Himself* (London, 1872), p. 35.

14 *Ibid.,* pp. 57–58, 63–64.

15 Thomas Cooper, *The Purgatory of Suicides, a Prison-Rhyme* (London, 1845). Also in *The Poetical Works of Thomas Cooper* (London, 1877), pp. 11–282. This long poem in Spenserian stanza contains eight stanzas addressed directly to Milton and ten more in which Milton serves as guide to Cooper on a second trip to Hades. See 1845 edition, Bk. II, sts. 8–19, pp. 53–57.

16 This note does not appear in the 1845 edition. It can be found, however, in the 1877 edition of the *Poetical Works,* p. 74.

17 In the *Daily Telegraph* (London), December 18, 1873.

18 Mark Pattison, *Milton* (London, 1879), p. 184.

19 See the New York *Tribune,* XXXVI (Tuesday, Sept. 19, 1876), 1; The New York *Sun,* XLIV (Tuesday, Sept. 19, 1876), [2].

20 Edward Hitchcock, *The Religion of Geology* (Boston, 1851), p. 80.

21 Charles Darwin, *Autobiography,* ed. Nora Barlow (New York, 1959), p. 85.

22 Frederic Harrison, "Poets that I Love," in *Among My Books* (London, 1912), pp. 63–64.

23 William Michael Rossetti, *Dante Gabriel Rossetti, His Family-Letters with a Memoir* (Boston, 1895), II, 5, 12.

24 John Milton, *Areopagitica,* in *Prose Selections,* ed. Merritt Y. Hughes (New York, 1947), p. 244.

25 This novel was first translated into English from the German of Max Ring by F. Jordan and was published in New York in 1868. Another English translation was done by John Jefferson, who published it in London and Manchester in 1889. Throughout the Notes, my references are to the American edition of 1868.

26 Max Ring, *John Milton and His Times* (New York, 1868), Bk. II, Chap. 2, pp. 132–33. For a listing of books pertaining to the Milton-Galileo meeting, see Marjorie Nicolson, "Milton and the Telescope," in *Science and Imagination* (Ithaca, 1956), p. 88, n. 11.

27 Major Vetch, *Milton at Rome, a Dramatic Piece* (Edinburg, 1851).

28 See David Masson, *The Life of John Milton* (New York, 1946). Masson discusses the Leonora episode in Vol. I, 802–805. Milton's letter is quoted, I, 802.

29 John Milton, "Ad Leonoram Romae Canentem," in *Minor Poems,* pp. 298–302.

30 Edward George Bulwer-Lytton, "Milton," in *The Siamese Twins and Other Poems* (New York, 1831), p. 255.

31 *Milton and His Times,* pp. 136–39.

32 Anne Manning, *Mary Powell and Deborah's Diary,* Everyman's Library edition.

33 Mrs. Anna Brownell (Murphy) Jameson, *Memoirs of the Loves of the Poets* (Boston and New York, 1888). See Chap. 19, pp. 249–63. The book, which was often reprinted, was first published under the title *Loves of the Poets* (London, 1829).

34 George Eliot, *Middlemarch,* World's Classics edition, pp. 5, 301.

35 Peter Bayne, "Milton," *Contemporary Review,* XXII (1873), 447.

36 Macaulay, "Milton," in *Essays,* I, 152. Cf. Henry, Lord Brougham, who, in a speech, once declared that Milton was "the greatest genius, which this country, or Europe, has in modern times produced."—*Speeches of Henry Lord Brougham* (4 vols., Edinburgh, 1838), I, 340.

37 Robert Willmott, "The Life of John Milton," in *Lives of Sacred Poets, Second Series* (London, 1838), p. 3.

38 Richard Hurrell Froude, *Remains* (London, 1838), I, 177.

39 Gerard Manley Hopkins, *The Letters of Gerard Manley Hopkins to Robert Bridges,* ed. Claude Colleer Abbott (London, 1955), Letter XXX, April 3, 1877, p. 39.

II. SHAKESPEARE AND MILTON

1 Samuel Taylor Coleridge, *Biographia Literaria,* in *Works,* III, 381.

2 In England, the "two schools" approach reached the proportions of a fad. For example, Mark Pattison described poetry as either "naive" or "artificial" in his essay on Milton in *The English Poets,* ed. Thomas H. Ward (New York, 1908), II, 301. John Keble, the Professor of Poetry at Oxford during the 1830's, drew a distinction between "primary" and "secondary" poets in his review of the "Life and Writings of Sir Walter Scott," *British Critic and Quarterly Theological Review,* XXIV (1838), 426–27, 439. See also Aubrey de Vere, "The Two Chief Schools of English Poetry," in *Essays Chiefly on Poetry* (London, 1887), II, 107, 110.

3 Friedrich Schiller, "On Naive and Sentimental Poetry," in *Works,* VIII, 287.

4 *Ibid.,* 285.

5 *Ibid.,* 292, 323.

6 See Martin William Steinke's introduction to his edition of

Young's *Conjectures* (New York, 1917), p. 9. Here Steinke writes: "Shakespeare, like Milton, is discussed in [the *Conjectures*] principally as a modern man of genius who is not only equal but even superior to the ancients." Appendix I of this edition lists numerous statements prior to Young's treatise in which various critics speak of the imagination and original genius of Milton and Shakespeare in much the same terms.

7   It is possible that Schiller was influenced by Young and other eighteenth-century critics through Hamaan and Herder, who were far more interested in Young's *Conjectures* than were English critics. See, for instance, Steinke's introduction to *Conjectures on Original Composition,* pp. 14–15.

8   Schiller, *Works,* VIII, 287–88.

9   Coleridge, *Works,* III, 381. Although Coleridge knew Schiller's essay "On Naive and Sentimental Poetry," I only wish to suggest here the similarity between the two critics' attitudes toward Shakespeare and Milton. For evidence that Coleridge knew Schiller's essay, see Frederick Ewen, *The Prestige of Schiller in England* (New York, 1932); *The Notebooks of Samuel Taylor Coleridge,* 2 vols., ed. Kathleen Coburn (New York, 1957), I, *entry* 1705, 16.92(i) for December, 1803.

10 Coleridge was so profoundly alive to the particular artistic powers of both Shakespeare and Milton that it was always difficult for him to think of one as superior to the other. Speaking of Shakespeare's "stupendous power," Coleridge makes it clear that it seats him not above but "on one of the glory-smitten summits of the poetic mountain, with Milton as his compeer not rival."—*Biographia Literaria, Works,* III, 381.

11 William Hazlitt, *Works,* V, 47.

12 *Ibid.,* VIII, 42.

13 *Ibid.,* V, 230.

14 *Ibid.,* V, 47.

15 *Ibid.,* V, 57. Also cf. Leigh Hunt, who in *Imagination and Fancy* (London, 1845), pp. 237–38, declared that Milton "had no pretensions to Shakespeare's universality." Peter Bayne, a later Victorian critic, grew eloquent in propounding a similar view. To him Milton "was not of that class of poets . . . for whom concrete men and women in their whole range of character, from sage to simpleton, from saint to sot, from ape to archangel are endlessly interesting; who are not uncontrollably fired with reforming ardour; who do not expect the world to become much better than it is." Consequently, as Shakespeare is "the supreme name" in the

"order of poets, the men of sympathy and of humour, Milton stands first in that other great order which is too didactic for humour, and of which Schiller is the best recent representative."— "Milton," *Contemporary Review,* XXII, 430–31. Likewise, George Saintsbury wrote that if Milton "falls short of Homer, Dante, and Shakespeare, it is chiefly because he expresses less of that humanity, both universal and quintessential, which they, and especially the last, put into verse. Narrowness is his fault."—*A History of Elizabethan Literature* (London, 1901), pp. 329–30.

16 Thomas Carlyle, *Works,* XXV, 90–91.

17 The already committed Arnold, yearning for "the calm, the cheerfulness, the disinterested objectivity" of early Greek genius, denounced the "many critics of the present day" who inveigh "against subjects chosen from distant times and countries," and demand modern subjects. He quoted with scorn "an intelligent critic" who, writing in a contemporary issue of *The Spectator,* stated that "the Poet who would really fix the public attention must leave the exhausted past, and draw his subjects from matters of present import, and *therefore* both of interest and novelty."— Preface to *Poems: 1853* in *The Poetical Works of Matthew Arnold,* ed. C. B. Tinker and H. F. Lowry (New York, 1950), p. xix.

J. A. St. John, in his Preface to the Bohn Library edition of Milton's Prose, is typical of Victorian critics who applauded the poets' involvement in current affairs. "Nothing, in fact, can be more unwise," he wrote, "than to desire that pure and lofty minds should keep themselves aloof from the world and the world's business. . . . Poets should never forget they are men and citizens." St. John praises Milton, who engaged himself in "matters of present import." Milton, he says, "had a view to the public good" in everything he wrote; "and, in fact, regarded the promotion of this to the utmost as so much his duty, that, in his contest with the bishops, he urges as his principal motive, the undying reproaches of conscience to which silence and tame submission would have exposed him."—*The Prose Works,* I (London, 1848), ii, vii–viii.

III. THE MILTONIC SONNET

1 Schiller, "On Naive and Sentimental Poetry," in *Works,* VIII, 288.
2 David Masson, "Shakespeare and Goethe," in *Essays,* p. 8.

3 *Ibid.,* pp. 11–12.

4 See Shakespeare, *The Sonnets,* New Variorum Edition, ed. Hyder E. Rollins (2 vols., Philadelphia, 1944), II, 133–34.

5 Masson, "Shakespeare and Goethe," in *Essays,* p. 12. Cf. Thomas Carlyle: "Doubt it not, he [Shakespeare] had his own sorrows: those *Sonnets* of his will even testify expressly in what deep waters he had waded." *Heroes, Hero-Worship and the Heroic in History,* in *Works,* V, 108.

6 See Pattison's Introduction to *The Sonnets of John Milton* (New York, 1896), p. 39.

7 William Shakespeare, *Supplement to the edition of "Shakespeare's plays,"* published in 1778 by Samuel Johnson and George Stee-vens . . .; with notes by the editor [Edmond Malone] and others (2 vols., London, 1780), I, 682–84.

8 Samuel Johnson, ed., *A Dictionary of the English Language* (2 vols., London, 1795), II, s.v. "Sonnet."

9 Despite disapproval of major critics, lesser poetic figures used the sonnet form extensively during the later eighteenth century. See Lawrence J. Zillman, *John Keats and the Sonnet Tradition* (Los Angeles, 1939), pp. 36–42.

10 Whereas Petrarch's sonnets almost always contained two enclosed, self-contained quatrains and two tercets, the final tercet rarely ending with a couplet, the Elizabethan sonneteers hardly ever adhered to this pattern. Moreover, the Elizabethans often completely disregarded or freely varied the Petrarchan rhyme scheme. Milton, however, continued to employ the Petrarchan pattern of rhyme. Charles Tomlinson, in *The Sonnet, Its Origin, Structure and Place in Poetry* (London, 1874), pp. 74–75, said: "The best English sonnets, according to the Italian type, are, in my opinion, those of Milton. . . . Although Milton does not always close his second quatrain with a full point, and is not sufficiently varied in his rhymes, he is closer to the Italian type than any other English poet."

11 James Glassford, in his *Lyrical Compositions selected from the Italian Poets* (Edinburgh, 1846), pp. 587-88, was the first critic to notice how closely Milton's sonnets correspond to Della Casa's in this respect. "It is evident," he wrote, "how much Milton profited in the formation of his style by his acquaintance with the Italian poets, and his familiar knowledge of their lyrical writers; and to none, it may be presumed, more than to Della Casa, who may fairly be looked upon as his prototype."

12 James Glassford in his Introduction to the *Lyrical Compositions,*

pp. v-vi, complained that the collections of Italian sonnets previously made were filled with "numerous pieces . . . which, from their trivial character, and, in some cases, even immoral tendency, might well have been allowed to pass into oblivion." His purpose, therefore, was "to make choice of such only as are altogether free from this last objection. . . . But all of them . . . will be found blameless in thought and expression, and the greater part to have the farther and higher recommendation of embodying some just sentiment or important truth."

13 Hazlitt, "On Milton's Sonnets," in *Works,* VIII, 174–75.

14 Charles Lamb, "Some Sonnets of Sir Philip Sidney," in *The Works of Charles and Mary Lamb,* ed. E. V. Lucas (7 vols., London, 1903), II, 213.

15 Henry Hallam, *Introduction to the Literature of Europe* (New York, 1863), III, 256, 263–64.

16 James Ashcroft Noble, "The Sonnet in England," *Contemporary Review,* XXXVIII (September, 1880), 459.

17 Macaulay, "Milton," in *Essays,* I, 170–71. A. W. Verity in his Introduction to *Milton's Sonnets* (Cambridge, 1916 [first edition, 1895]), note to p. xxx, said that "to Macaulay belongs the credit of being one of the first (if not *the* first) of prose-critics to do justice to Milton's Sonnets and reverse the eighteenth-century verdict, as expressed by Johnson and Steevens."

18 James Montgomery, "Memoir of John Milton," in *The Poetical Works of John Milton* (New York, n.d.), I, xxix.

19 Noble, "The Sonnet in England," *Contemporary Review,* XXXVIII, 459.

20 Quoted from a MS by S. M. Paraclita Reilly in *Aubrey De Vere* (Lincoln, Nebr., 1953), p. 98.

21 See Sir Aubrey de Vere, *Sonnets* (London, 1875), pp. xiii–xiv.

22 "A Talk about Sonnets," *Blackwood's Edinburgh Magazine,* CXXVIII (August, 1880), 159.

23 *Ibid.,* pp. 163–64.

24 Tennyson, whose sonnets are often very irregular, once lashed out against the critics when his brother Charles's sonnets were criticized for not being in perfect Petrarchan form: "I never care to read a perfect sonnet. I look down the rhymes and that's enough. I thought the other day of writing a sonnet beginning—I hate the Perfect Sonnet!" Quoted in *The Diary of William Allingham* (London, 1907), p. 302.

25 Pattison, *Milton's Sonnets,* pp. 11–13. Coventry Patmore also objected to the epigrammatic quality: "The sonnets of most English

poets are merely serious epigrams, with all the weight in the last line. Milton and Mr. Wordsworth have been better aware of the true spirit of this measure, which is the very reverse of epigrammatic."—"In Memoriam," *North British Review,* XIII (August, 1850), 539.

26 Pattison, *Milton's Sonnets,* p. 14.

27 *Ibid.,* p. 45.

28 *Ibid.,* pp. 34–35.

29 *Ibid.,* pp. 45–46.

30 Glassford, in his discussion of Della Casa's sonnets, praised rather than condemned Della Casa and Milton for adopting the freer sentence arrangement which Pattison was later to condemn. Noticing Della Casa's peculiar style, Glassford pointed out that in the construction of his sonnets, Della Casa customarily carried on "the sense from the close of one line to the beginning or middle of that which follows, thus suspending the attention of the reader, and avoiding the monotony which is produced by a uniform termination of the sentence at the close of the line or couplet. The advantage is not merely to give a relief by the varieties of the pause, but often to add much force and grandeur to the sentiment itself, by arresting the reader at a place and time unexpected, and forcing him, as it were, to halt for a moment and consider. In this manner his compositions possess, as to their style, both the beauty of rhyme and the solemnity and varied cadence of blank verse."—*Lyrical Compositions,* p. 587.

31 Pattison, *Milton's Sonnets,* pp. 54–55.

32 [Francis Jeffrey], Review of *Poems* by Wordsworth, *Edinburgh Review,* XI (October, 1807), 230.

33 George W. Sanderlin, "The Influence of Milton and Wordsworth on the Early Victorian Sonnet," *JELH,* V (September, 1938), 230.

34 *Ibid.,* p. 236.

35 "A Talk about Sonnets," *Blackwood's Edinburgh Magazine,* CXXVIII, 167.

36 See the Second Conversation between Southey and Porson, in *Works,* V, 181. Landor in the guise of Porson goes on to speak of Shakespeare's poems, "which are printed as sonnets," and declares that they lack imagination. "Even the interest we take in the private life of this miraculous man cannot keep the volume in our hands long together. We acknowledge great power, but we experience great weariness. Were I a poet, I would much rather have written the *Allegro* or the *Penseroso* than all those. . . ."

37 Pattison, *Milton's Sonnets,* p. 60.

38 Noble, "The Sonnet in England," *Contemporary Review,* XXXVIII, 451. Similarly, Edwin Paxton Hood speaks of the "rugged spiritual grandeur" and the "profound feeling" of Milton's sonnets in his chapter on the sonnets in *John Milton: the Patriot and Poet* (London, 1852). See Chapter XII, p. 140.

39 This is the only poem in either the 1830 or 1832 volume which shows Tennyson's keen interest in liberal political movements. See Charles Tennyson, *Six Tennyson Essays* (London, 1954), p. 41. Other early sonnets of a political nature which show Miltonic influence are "to J. M. K.," "Alexander," "'Buonoparte," and "How long, O God." See Dugal B. MacEachen, "Tennyson and the Sonnet," *Victorian Newsletter,* No. 14 (Fall, 1958), p. 2.

40 George Milner, "A Note on Two Sonnets by Milton and Tennyson," *Manchester Quarterly,* XI (1892), 356–59.

41 See R. D. Havens, *The Influence of Milton on English Literature* (Cambridge, Mass., 1922), p. 544; and Sanderlin, "The Influence of Milton and Wordsworth . . .," *JELH,* V, 239–40.

42 "Cyriack, this three years' Day," in *Minor Poems,* p. 397.

43 Albert Morton Turner, "Rossetti's Reading and His Critical Opinions," *PMLA,* XLII (1927), 475.

44 Quoted in Dorothy Stuart, *Christina Rossetti* (London, 1930), p. 106. Swinburne's words also may be relevant. The disciples of Dante, he said, allow no other gods on Parnassus; while "A Shakespearean adept may be a Miltonic believer," a Dante worshipper excludes all others from his view. "For these Unitarians or Mahametans of Parnassus there is but one Muse, and Dante is her prophet. . . . Most especially may we not offer sacrifice to any other great Christian or cosmogenic poet such as Milton; for in him is the whole and sole theogony revealed by spiritual song. This is a hard saying, and I for one cannot hear it."—*The Complete Works of Swinburne,* ed. Gosse and Wise (20 vols., London, 1926), XIV, 109.

45 Quoted in T. Hall Caine, *Recollections* (London, 1883), p. 237.

46 Another interesting example of late Victorian political sonnets in the Miltonic tradition is the work of Sir William Watson, one of the most popular poets of the 1890's. See, for instance, his *Ver Tenebrosum,* which appeared in the *National Review* for June, 1885, and his volume of sonnets, *The Purple East* (London, 1896).

47 First published in Charles Tennyson, "Tennyson's Unpublished Poems," *Nineteenth Century,* CIX (1931), 505–506. J. F. A. Pyre in *The Formation of Tennyson's Style* (Madison, 1921), p. 242,

also sees "extensive indebtedness for imagery to *Paradise Lost*" in several other early sonnets: "Shall the Hag Evil die," "The Pallid thunderstricken sigh," and the three sonnets entitled "Love" which appeared in the 1830 volume and later were not reprinted. These sonnets are in Tennyson, *Works,* p. 785.

48 This passage also is very reminiscent of James Thomson's *The Seasons,* especially "Winter," *passim.*

49 See W. H. Gardner, *Gerard Manley Hopkins* (2 vols., London, 1948), I, 97. For texts of these poems, see *The Note-books and Papers of Gerard Manley Hopkins,* ed. Humphry House (London and New York, 1937), pp. 42–44. Also see Hopkins' letter to his mother, 1 March 1877, in *Further Letters of Gerard Manley Hopkins,* ed. Claude Colleer Abbott (London, 1956), p. 144.

50 See *The Letters of Gerard Manley Hopkins to Robert Bridges,* ed. Claude Colleer Abbott (London, 1955), p. 37, and Albert J. Guerard, *Robert Bridges* (Cambridge, Mass., 1942), p. 46.

51 Hazlitt, *Works,* VIII, 180.

IV. THE RELIGIOUS EPIC AND THE MILTONIC SUBLIME

1 John Wilson, *Noctes Ambrosianae* (4 vols., Edinburgh and London, 1856), III, 235. This selection originally appeared in *Blackwood's Edinburgh Magazine,* XXX (April, 1831).

2 George Gilfillan, "John Milton," in *A Second Gallery of Literary Portraits* (Edinburgh, 1850), p. 26.

3 George Meredith, "The Poetry of Milton," in *The Poetical Works of George Meredith* (New York, 1912), p. 15.

4 Robert Montgomery, *Satan, a Poem* (London, 1830), p. 248.

5 See Marjorie Nicolson's discussion of the two sublimes in *Mountain Gloom and Mountain Glory* (Ithaca, 1959), pp. 29–31. Miss Nicolson's book, which discusses the development of the Aesthetics of the Infinite, especially Chapter Seven, is basic to my discussion of the natural Sublime in this chapter.

6 John Dennis, "The Grounds of Criticism in Poetry," in *The Critical Works of John Dennis,* 2 vols. (Baltimore, 1939), I, 338.

7 *Ibid.,* p. 340.

8 *Ibid.,* p. 361.

9 Joseph Addison, *The Spectator* (4 vols., New York, n.d.), III, No. 412, p. 59.

10 Dennis, "Grounds of Criticism," in *Critical Works,* I, 351.

11 See George Gilfillan's account of Edward Irving in *Literary Por-*

traits (Edinburgh, 1845), pp. 130–57, and "Edward Irving" in *A Third Gallery of Portraits* (Edinburgh, 1854), especially p. 45. Also see Andrew L. Drummond, *Edward Irving and His Circle* (London, [1937]), especially Chap. 3, "The Celebrated Irving."

12 Drummond, *Edward Irving and His Circle,* p. 115.

13 "John Milton versus Robert Montgomery," *Knickerbocker Magazine,* III (1834), 122.

14 Elmer Edgar Stoll, "Milton a Romantic," *RES,* VIII (1932), 425. Stoll's view was often anticipated by nineteenth-century critics. Cf., for instance, Hood, *John Milton,* p. 167. In describing the sublime universe of Milton's *Paradise Lost* he said: "The mind of the reader is constantly on the stretch. . . . Thus we find how constantly Milton's mind was crowded with the sublimest objects. Size, and dimension appear to have most impressed him." Similarly, the author of "Milton and His Epic," *Sharpe's London Magazine,* n.s., VI (1855), 309, said, "But his particular cast or direction was towards the stupendous and the Sublime. His mind dwelt, as in its native region, in the infinite." Milton's mind, he continued, was "Alp-like in the towering grandeur of its original endowments." Cf. Francis Thompson, "John Milton," *The Academy,* LI (27 March 1897), 357.

15 For details of Martin's life and work, see Thomas Balston, *John Martin, His Life and Works* (London, 1947).

16 See Thomas Balston, "John Martin, 1789–1854, Illustrator and Pamphleteer," *Transactions of the Bibliographical Society,* Second Series, XIV (1934), 391–92. Balston says that in 1828 "Martin supplied a frontispiece to *The Fall of Nineveh, a Poem* by his friend Edwin Atherstone. In the same year Martin had shown at the British Institution his large picture of this title, of which he published an engraving in 1830. Both the poet in his Preface and Martin in his descriptive catalogue of the picture disclaim any collaboration beyond mutual discussions of the subject. In the following year Atherstone, under the pretense of reviewing Alan Cunningham's *Lives of the Most Eminent British Painters, Sculptors, and Architects,* published in the *Edinburgh Review* an article which is entirely about Martin." Balston also mentions other instances.

17 See Frederick Antal, *Fuseli Studies* (London, 1956), p. 148. Antal says that the pictures of Martin "signified a popularisation, one might almost say an unconsciously low-brow debasement, of scenes of terror taken from Fuseli and also from Turner into pseudo-realistic melodramatic romanticism." Martin often treated Fuseli

themes similarly, such as *Macbeth* and *Paradise Lost.* "Generally speaking," Antal continues, "he was a favourite painter with princes, with writers of novels of terror like Bulwer-Lytton, with the large number of upper middle-class people who had lower middle-class taste and presumably with the lower middle-class itself. He was probably the most internationally famous English painter of his time."

18 Balston, *John Martin,* Chap. 12, "1824–8. First Mezzotints. Paradise Lost," pp. 94–105. See also Kester Svendsen's remarks about Martin in his recent article, "John Martin and the Explusion Scene of *Paradise Lost,*" *Studies in English Literature, 1500-1900,* I (1961), 63–73.

19 Balston, "John Martin, Illustrator," *Transactions of the Bibliographical Society,* Second Series, XIV, 389–90. That Martin's contemporaries were especially impressed by the natural Sublime in his paintings is indicated in verses such as this one from "To John Martin, on his Magnificent print of Joshua," by Bernard Barton (*A New Year's Eve,* 1828):

> Vistas of unbounded space,
> Architecture's richest grace,
> Lurid clouds by lightnings riven,
> Conflict fierce on earth, in heaven!

20 For details of Fuseli's life and works, see two recent studies: Paul Ganz, *The Drawings of Henry Fuseli* (New York, 1949), and Frederick Antal, *Fuseli Studies.*

21 Antal, *Fuseli Studies,* pp. 28–29.

22 *Ibid.,* pp. 84–85.

23 See Ganz, *The Drawings of Henry Fuseli,* Plates #18 and #86.

24 Robert Pollok, *The Course of Time* (Edinburgh and London, 1827), Bk. II, 253.

25 G. S. R. Kitson Clark, "The Romantic Element—1830 to 1850," *Studies in Social History* (London, 1955), p. 225.

26 "Milton versus Montgomery," *Knickerbocker Magazine,* III, 120. The anonymous reviewer also noted that Montgomery took pleasure in being styled the "modern Milton" (p. 124), but he went on to say that Montgomery's desire to challenge Milton on his own ground was "the daring of stupidity."

27 [William Maginn], "Mr. Robert Montgomery's 'Satan,'" *Fraser's Magazine,* I (February, 1830), 95–99. The second article is a review of "The Descent into Hell," *Fraser's Magazine,* I (April, 1830), 341–52. For proof of Maginn's authorship, see Miriam

Thrall, *Rebellious Fraser's* (New York, 1934), p. 101. On the same page, Miss Thrall notes that one of the poets Maginn pursues through the early volumes of *Fraser's* is the "youthful homilist," Robert Montgomery, who "had been widely hailed by his fellow poets as a coming Milton, and the beauty and profundity of his work was already considered established."

28 [Thomas Macaulay], "Mr. Robert Montgomery's *Poems,* and the Modern Practice of Puffing," *Edinburgh Review,* LI (April, 1830), 193–210.

29 [Maginn], "Mr. Robert Montgomery's 'Satan,' " *Fraser's Magazine,* I, 95.

30 Macaulay's attitude toward Martin is made clear in his review of "The Pilgrim's Progress, with a Life of John Bunyan," *Edinburgh Review,* LIV (December, 1831), 450. I quote: "It is with unfeigned diffidence that we pronounce judgment on any question relating to the art of painting. But it appears to us that Mr. Martin has not of late been fortunate in his choice of subjects. He should never have attempted to illustrate *Paradise Lost.* There can be no two manners more directly opposed to each other than the manner of his painting and the manner of Milton's feeling. Those things which are merely accessory in the descriptions become the principal objects in the pictures; and those figures which are most prominent in the descriptions can be detected in the pictures only by a close scrutiny."

31 [Macaulay], "Mr. Robert Montgomery's *Poems,*" *Edinburgh Review,* LI, 209.

32 "Montgomery's *Satan,*" *Athenaeum,* 9 January 1830, pp. 1–2.

33 [Maginn], "The Descent into Hell," *Fraser's Magazine,* I, 341–42.

34 *Ibid.,* p. 343.

35 *Ibid.,* p. 349. See also pp. 350–51. Maginn, of course, was not the only reviewer impressed by Heraud's *Descent.*

36 [John Wilson], "The Fall of Nineveh," *Blackwood's Edinburgh Magazine,* XXVII (February, 1830), 137–72.

37 *Ibid.,* p. 137.

38 *Ibid.,* p. 144.

39 *Ibid.,* pp. 145–46.

40 *Ibid.,* p. 172.

41 "Reade's Poems," *Edinburgh Review,* LIII (March, 1831), 105–119. (Probably but not certainly by Macaulay.)

42 *Ibid.,* p. 105.

43 *Ibid.,* p. 107.

44 *Ibid.,* p. 109.

45 *Ibid.,* p. 110.

46 In commenting on John Martin's abilities, Edwin Atherstone in his review of *Lives of the Most Eminent British Painters* which appeared in the *Edinburgh Review,* XLIX (June, 1829), 465, says that Martin's genius is "essentially Epic . . . he can work with Homer, or with Milton, in presenting a great event, with all its magnificent concurrents—the confusion and rage of battle—physical sublimity, darkness and tempest; but he can do nothing with Shakespeare, in embodying the passion of Love, or the fine philosophy and solemn musings of Hamlet."

47 [John Wilson], "Dies Borealis," No. 9, *Blackwood's Edinburgh Magazine,* LXXII (August, 1852), 140–41.

48 John Abraham Heraud, *The Judgement of the Flood* (London, 1834), Preface, the pages of which are not numbered.

49 Quoted from a review in *The Times* in an anonymous review of *The Diety* in *Eclectic Review,* Third Series, XII (November, 1834), 360.

50 Nicolson, *Mountain Gloom,* p. 273.

51 In Edith Heraud, *Memoirs of John A. Heraud* (London, 1898), p. 30.

52 Addison, *The Spectator,* III, No. 412, p. 59.

53 Montgomery, *Satan,* p. 345.

54 Edwin Atherstone, *The Fall of Nineveh* (London, 1828).

55 Robert Montgomery, "A Vision of Hell," in *A Universal Prayer; Death; A Vision of Heaven,* 2nd ed. (London, 1829), pp. 93, 96.

56 Robert Montgomery, *The Omnipresence of the Deity* (London, 1830), p. 26.

57 Nicolson in *Mountain Gloom,* p. 274, says that "in *Paradise Regained* the blind Milton's imagination carried over to earth the sense of vastness he had felt in the cosmos. The most extensive terrestrial panoramas of the seventeenth century are those Satan showed Christ from a mountain-top." Also see her article, "Milton and the Telescope," in *Science and Imagination* (Ithaca, 1956), especially pp. 93–94.

58 Robert Montgomery, *The Messiah* (London, 1832), pp. 104–105.

59 "Satan," *Monthly Review,* XIII (February, 1830), 159.

60 "Satan," *Gentleman's Magazine,* C (January, 1830), 43.

61 Thomas Ragg, *The Deity* (London, 1834), p. 1.

62 Gilfillan, "John Milton," in *A Second Gallery,* p. 27.

63 Percy B. Shelley, "On the Devil, and Devils," in *Works,* VI, 402. Cf. also Hood, *John Milton,* p. 171; Stanhope Busby, *Lectures on English Poetry* (London, 1837), pp. 95–96.

64 Hazlitt, "On Shakespeare and Milton," in *Works,* V, 63.
65 David Masson, "The Three Devils: Luther's, Milton's, and Goethe's," in *Essays,* p. 80. Cf. Hood, *John Milton,* pp. 164–65: "It is the intellectual, the internal character of Satan, which makes him an object of profound interest."
66 Hazlitt, *Works,* V, 63.
67 Masson, "Three Devils," in *Essays,* p. 63.
68 *Ibid.,* p. 61.
69 Hazlitt, *Works,* V, 63.
70 Masson, "Three Devils," in *Essays,* p. 62.
71 [John Wilson], "Dies Borealis," No. 9, *Blackwood's,* LXXII, 152.
72 Gilfillan, "John Milton," in *A Second Gallery,* p. 23.
73 Masson, "Three Devils," in *Essays,* p. 55.
74 Keightley, *John Milton,* p. 410.
75 "Satan," *Athenaeum,* 9 January 1830, p. 1.
76 [John Abraham Heraud], *The Descent into Hell* (London, 1830), p. 206.
77 William Blake, "The Marriage of Heaven and Hell," in *Poetry and Prose of William Blake,* ed. Geoffrey Keynes (New York, 1948), p. 182.
78 Walter Raleigh, *John Milton* (London, 1900), p. 132.
79 Walter Bagehot, "Wordsworth, Tennyson, and Browning," in *Literary Studies* (New York, n.d.), II, 321. Some who sympathized most with Satan cited the "Begat" passage (*Paradise Lost,* V, 600–615) to show that God was a tyrant and Satan was justified in refusing to obey the newly "begotten" Son. For instance, Walter Bagehot in his review of David Masson's biography of Milton (printed as "John Milton" in *Literary Studies,* I, 188), anticipated Denis Saurat in interpreting the word "begot" (1. 603) to mean literally "created" or "generated," and, therefore, felt that Satan was slighted and abused by having a newly created being placed above him for no good reason. Consequently, Abdiel's contention that the Son existed before the angels and participated in their creation is untrue: " *'This day'* he [the Son] seems to have come into existence, and could hardly have assisted at the creation of the angels, who are not young, and who converse with one another like old acquaintances." See the whole discussion of this passage, I, 185–90.
80 Shelley, *Works,* VI, 388.
81 Bagehot, "Wordsworth, Tennyson, and Browning," in *Literary Studies,* II, 321. Modern criticism has strongly repudiated the Shelleyan concept of Milton's Satan. See, for instance, F. M.

Krouse, *Milton's Samson and the Christian Tradition* (Princeton, 1949), and Elizabeth Pope, *Paradise Regained; the Tradition and the Poem* (Baltimore, 1947).

82 In his chapter entitled "Milton's Satan," Hood declared: "in painting Satan, the poet painted himself: this sublime and daring determination was a portion of his soul,—that sublime resolution, undaunted, defiant of the bellowing thunder, the surging fires, and the swift, fierce lightnings, was but the painting of the reality with which Milton himself went forth to encounter the terrible hurricanes of life."—*John Milton*, p. 158.

83 Masson, "Three Devils," in *Essays Biographical and Critical*, p. 64.

84 Stenographer's transcript of lecture in Fernande Tardivel, *La Personnalité littéraire de Newman* (Paris, 1937), p. 389.

85 F. A. Cox, "Milton's *Paradise Lost*," *Journal of Sacred Literature*, I (April, 1848), 255. Walter Bagehot believed that the great error in *Paradise Lost* is the fact that Milton made Satan "interesting." However, he declared that when Milton wrote *Paradise Lost* he "was not conscious of the effect his teaching would produce in an age like this, when scepticism is in the air, and when it is not possible to help looking coolly on his delineations. Probably in our boyhood we can recollect a period when any solemn description of celestial events would have commanded our respect; we should not have dared to read it intelligently, to canvass its details and see what it meant: it was a religious book; it sounded reverential, and that would have sufficed. Something like this was the state of mind of the seventeenth century."—"John Milton," *Literary Studies*, I, 188.

86 John Ruskin, *Works*, XI, 174. Cf. Hazlitt, *Works*, V, 65: "Milton was too magnanimous and open an antagonist [of Satan] to support his argument by the bye-tricks of a hump and cloven foot. . . . He relied on the justice of his cause, and did not scruple to give the devil his due." Hazlitt, therefore, disagreed with those persons who thought Milton had "carried his liberality too far, and injured the cause he professed to espouse by making him [Satan] the chief person in his poem." Also see [John Wilson], "Dies Borealis," No. 10, *Blackwood's Edinburgh Magazine*, LXXII, 376. Here Wilson listed three things which "necessitated Satan's poetical exaltation in Books First and Second." He concluded that the reader follows Satan's progress "certainly *not* desiring success, by which we are to suffer, but with eyes that are fixed upon him by curiosity, by pity, for so much good that remains in him of

what he was, by admiration of what is in him of yet unextinguished greatness."

87 Masson, "Three Devils," in *Essays,* p. 83.

88 Raleigh, *Milton,* p. 83. Lines quoted are from *Paradise Regained,* I, 412–15.

89 See "William Herbert's Imitation of Milton," *Monthly Review,* CXLV (1838), 392–93.

90 For a complete study of the 1839 *Festus,* see Morse Peckham, "Guilt and Glory: A study of the 1839 *Festus,*" Ph.D. thesis, Princeton University, 1947.

91 Charles Kingsley, *Literary and General Lectures and Essays* (London, 1890), p. 51.

92 Phillip James Bailey, "A Spiritual Legend," in *The Mystic and Other Poems* (Boston, 1856), p. 72.

93 Havens, *The Influence of Milton,* p. 233n.

94 Balston, "John Martin, Illustrator," *Transactions of the Bibliographical Society,* Second Series, XIV, 407.

V. MILTON THE PURITAN: PRO AND CON

1 See, for example, Malcolm Ross's reading of Milton in *Milton's Royalism* (Ithaca, 1943).

2 Peter Bayne, "Milton," in *The Chief Actors in the Puritan Revolution* (London, 1879), p. 299.

3 Ruskin, *Works,* XXIII, 277.

4 Wilson, *Noctes Ambrosianae,* I, 34.

5 Matthew Arnold, "A French Critic on Milton," in *Mixed Essays* (London, 1903), p. 244.

6 Samuel Johnson, "John Milton," in *Lives of the English Poets,* Everyman's Library edition, I, 93.

7 T. S. Eliot, "Milton I" (1936), in *On Poetry and Poets* (New York, 1957), p. 156. Although Eliot modified his position on Milton the poet in the 1947 Milton essay (pp. 165–83 in *On Poetry*), he did not change his opinion of Milton's character. In fact, he expressed hope that he, unlike Dr. Johnson, would not allow his "antipathy towards Milton the man" (p. 168) to influence his judgment of Milton's poetry.

8 See William Haller, *The Rise of Puritanism* (New York, 1957), p. 156.

9 Lucy Hutchinson, *Memoirs of the Life of Colonel Hutchinson* (2 vols., London, 1885), I, 112 ff.

10   [David Masson], review of *The Works of John Milton, North British Review,* XVI (February, 1852), 304.

11   "The Youth of Milton," *Edinburgh Review,* CXI (April, 1860), 316.

12   Cyrus R. Edmonds, *John Milton* (London, 1851), pp. iii–iv. Hood in his preface to *John Milton* claimed to eschew bias of any kind and made it clear that in his biography "the true opinions of England's greatest son," the man of God who "should be the darling, the Eikon Basilike of all young men," are presented "without the veilings and trammellings of sectarianism" (p. ix).

13   Robert Fletcher, "An Introductory Review," in *The Prose Works of John Milton* (London, 1835), p. iv. William Carpenter in his *Life and Times of John Milton* (London, 1836), p. 16, referred to this as "Mr. Fletcher's compendious, elegant, and cheap edition of Milton's Prose Works" and declared Fletcher's estimate of Milton's character to be "much juster" than that of Egerton Brydges in his *Life of Milton.*

14   Fletcher, "Introductory Review," in *Prose Works of John Milton,* p. v. Also cf. Hood, *John Milton,* Chap. 13, "Milton and Johnson": "For a very long time the life of Milton most referred to, and most frequently reprinted, was that by Dr. Johnson, the most malevolent piece of Biography ever penned" (p. 145).

15   Joseph Ivimey, *John Milton* (New York, 1833), p. viii. A copy of the "Animadversions" is attached to this edition of the biography.

16   Review of Milton's *Works, Eclectic Magazine,* XXX (1853), 365.

17   Raleigh, *Milton,* p. 57.

18   Ivimey, *John Milton,* p. iii.

19   Carpenter, *John Milton,* p. iii.

20   Fletcher, "Introductory Review," in *Prose Works of John Milton,* p. ii.

21   *Ibid.,* p. i.

22   Carpenter, *John Milton,* p. iv.

23   Ivimey, *John Milton,* p. iv.

24   Hood, *John Milton,* p. x.

25   Carpenter, *John Milton,* p. 9.

26   Edmonds, *John Milton,* p. iv.

27   Ivimey, *John Milton,* p. iii.

28   Fletcher, "Introductory Review," in *Prose Works of John Milton,* p. ii.

29   Thomas Carlyle, in 1822, read the prose works in their entirety.

See *Two Notebooks of Thomas Carlyle, from 23rd March, 1822, to 16th May, 1832,* ed. Charles Eliot Norton (New York, 1898), entries for 15 April, 22 April, 6 May 1822, etc. Also it should be noted that Walter Savage Landor, who admired the courage and strength of conviction which Milton, "that steadfast patriot," exhibited, preferred the "heavy cut velvet" of Milton's prose, "with its ill-placed Roman fibula, to the spangled gauze and gummed-on flowers and puffy flounces of our present street-walking literature." See Carlyle, *Works,* V, 232, 235.

30 Fletcher, "Introductory Review," in *Prose Works of John Milton,* p. ii.

31 *Ibid.,* p. ii.

32 *Ibid.,* p. v.

33 Ivimey, *John Milton,* p. iv.

34 See Albert K. Stevens, "Milton and Chartism," *PQ,* XII (1933), 377–88. Also see the anonymous review, "Ernest, the Chartist Epic," *Quarterly Review,* LXV (1840), 190–91.

35 It should be noted that, despite widespread belief, especially in liberal circles, that Milton was a democrat, many Victorian critics were quite aware that this idea was utterly false. John Tulloch said in his essay on "Milton" in *English Puritanism and Its Leaders* (Edinburgh and London, 1861), p. 235, that while Milton was a republican, "he was no democrat. So far from this, his nature and all his sympathies were intensely aristocratical. It was not for the government of the people, the 'credulous and hapless herd begotten to servility,' but for the government of the *wisest,* that he cared."

Richard Garnett in his *Life of John Milton* (London, 1890), p. 120, likewise declared that "Milton was one of the innumerable proofs that a man may be very much of a Republican without being anything of a Liberal. He was as firm a believer in right divine as any Cavalier, save that in his view such right was vested in the worthiest."

Also see Raleigh, *Milton,* p. 58; Keightley, *John Milton,* p. 226; "Milton and the Commonwealth," *British Quarterly Review,* X (1 August, 1849), 250.

36 [David Masson], review of *The Works of John Milton, North British Review,* XVI, 335. Most of this essay is reprinted as "The Youth of Milton" in *Essays.*

37 Robert Wallace, "John Milton," in *Antitrinitarian Biography* (London, 1850), III, 328–29.

38 Edward Dowden, "Milton: Civil Liberty," in *Puritan and Anglican* (London, 1900), pp. 133–34.

39 Ivimey, *John Milton,* p. vi.

40 Raleigh, *Milton,* p. 69.

41 Soon after the appearance of Ivimey's biography, Sir Egerton Brydges published his *Life of Milton* (1833) which, despite its typical Tory-eighteenth century approach, was often reprinted during the Victorian period.

42 James Froude, "The Oxford Counter-Reformation," in *Short Studies of Great Subjects* (New York, 1908), V, 178.

43 Richard Hurrell Froude, *Remains,* I, 177. Also quoted in Louise Guiney, *Hurrell Froude* (London, 1904), p. 24.

44 Quoted in C. E. Byles, *The Life and Letters of Robert S. Hawker* (London and New York, 1905), p. 232. Also see Hawker's letter to Rev. W. West, January 23, 1855, *ibid.,* p. 239.

45 Thomas B. Macaulay, "A Conversation between Mr. Abraham Cowley and Mr. John Milton," in *Works,* VII, 652. This conversation first appeared in *Knight's Quarterly Magazine,* August, 1824.

46 Joseph Henry Shorthouse, *John Inglesant* (London, 1910), p. 82. First edition appeared in May, 1881.

47 *Ibid.,* p. 434.

48 William Morris, *The Collected Works of William Morris* (23 vols., London, 1914), XXII, xv. J. W. Mackail, in *The Life of William Morris* (2 vols., London, 1907), I, 219, wrote: "Milton he always abused, though he sometimes betrayed more knowledge of him than he would have been willing to admit." Cf. also Oliver Elton, *A Survey of English Literature* (2 vols., London, 1927), II, 51.

49 Samuel Roberts, *Milton Unmasked* (London, 1844), p. vii.

50 *Ibid.,* p. ix.

51 *Ibid.,* p. x.

52 *Ibid.,* p. 16.

53 *Ibid.,* p. 31. Roberts, like most of those who harbored a strong dislike for Milton, reported that the poet mistreated his wives and daughters. According to Roberts, during Mary Powell's absence from Milton's house, the young Milton "was endeavouring to seduce another respectable female to become the victim of his licentiousness till he should become tired of her." In the end, Mary was made to humble herself "in the dust before her tyrant" (p. 18).

This, of course, is an extreme example. But Milton was later taken to task by Victorians for his alleged mistreatment of the women in his family. Mrs. Leman Gillies, in her article, "Milton and his Daughters," which appeared in the *People's Journal,*

V (1848), 227, condemned Milton particularly for leaving his daughters uneducated. "When we behold his automaton daughters," she wrote, "reduced to mere reading machines, it is difficult to say which is the stronger feeling—compassion for them, or indignation towards him."

Peter Bayne, "John Milton," *Contemporary Review,* XXII, 447, remarked that "the grave Puritan displeasure with which Milton regarded the mother seems to have been transferred to the children. His austerity as a Puritan and a pedagogue, and the worse than old Hebrew meanness of his estimate of women, appear to the greatest disadvantage in connection with his daughters." For a recent version of this same untenable view, see Robert Graves's novel, *Wife to Mr. Milton* (New York, 1944). See also Thomas Keightley's refutation of this attitude in *John Milton,* pp. 89–91.

54 Blunt's reaction was but one of many different responses to Milton's *De Doctrina Christiana,* which was discovered in 1823 and translated from the Latin, edited, and published by Charles Sumner in 1825. Bishop Burgess, for instance, in his Preface to an edition of Milton's *Of True Religion* (re-titled *Protestant Union* and published in London, 1826), refused to believe that the *De Doctrina* was Milton's because of its antitrinitarian orientation. A different reaction is found in a letter to the editor of *The Christian Journal and Literary Register,* XI (1827), 105–106, in which a reader declared: "Once I knew Milton only, or chiefly, as a great poet . . . devoted to the cause of pure and undefiled religion: at least *I* saw nothing in any of his performances to lead me to question his soundness in the faith. But now what shall I say?"

Despite the immediate reaction to the *De Doctrina,* especially in the periodical press, Macaulay, I believe, was very close to the truth, when, in his famous review of the *De Doctrina,* he confidently stated that within a few more days, "this essay will follow the *Defensio Populi* to the dust and silence of the upper shelf." See "Milton," in *Essays,* I, 151. Milton's heretical notions were soon forgotten by most Victorians, even though a few theologians and religious groups, especially the Unitarians, continued to interpret, praise, or denounce Milton's theological views. Francis Mineka, in his chapter, "The Religious Press vs. John Milton, Heretic," in *The Dissidence of Dissent: The Monthly Repository* (Chapel Hill, 1944), discusses in detail the reaction in the periodicals to Milton's controversial work. For a more complete study, see Mineka's "The Critical Reception of Milton's *De Doctrina Christiana," University of Texas Studies in English* (1943), pp. 115–47. Ruth M. Kivette, in her dissertation, "'Milton on the Trinity" (Columbia University Ph.D. Thesis, 1960), like Mineka, cites many contemporary reviews, and shows that Milton's antitrinitarian views do not coincide with the theological concepts of historical Unitarianism as some Victorians thought they did.

55 J. J. Blunt, "Milton," in *Essays Contributed to the Quarterly Review* (London, 1860), p. 88. This article first appeared in the *Quarterly* in June, 1827.

56 W. L. Bowles, *The Life of Thomas Ken* (2 vols., London, 1830–31), I, 87, 156.

57 Arnold, "A French Critic," in *Mixed Essays*, pp. 243–44.

58 Rev. Henry Stebbing, "Memoir of Milton's Life and Writings," reprinted often in various editions of Milton's work. My notes refer to the Memoir in *The Complete Poetical Works of John Milton* (New York, 1845), pp. xi, xvi.

59. Walter Bagehot, "John Milton," in *Literary Studies*, I, 166.

60 *Ibid.,* p. 161. For a similar analysis, see H. A. Taine's *History of English Literature,* trans. from the French by N. Van Laun, 2 vols. (New York and Chicago, n.d.), I, 503–504. Taine said that a soul like Milton's, fortified against temptation and the lures of active life, is "like a diver in his bell; it passes through life as he passes through the sea, unstained but isolated."

61 Jonathan Richardson, *Explanatory Notes and Remarks on Milton's Paradise Lost.* I have used the text printed in Helen Darbishire's edition of *The Early Lives of Milton* (London, 1932), p. 212.

62 Tulloch, *English Puritanism and Its Leaders,* pp. 275–76.

63. *Ibid.,* p. 245.

64 Arnold, "A French Critic," in *Mixed Essays*, pp. 269–70.

65 [Masson], review of *The Works of John Milton, North British Review,* XVI, 298. Hood, in *John Milton,* p. 51, stated similar ideas: "Looking upon him now, he seems to be the image of his age; his mind was cast in a mould originally singularly stern; it was not Saxon, it was not Grecian, in its structure; his birthplace, England; his favourite studies of Grecian lore appeared to be only absorbed into a grand Hebraistic temperament of soul; he rises before us shrouded in the grand habiliments of the ancient prophet; he combines within himself the poet, the prophet, the martyr, and the priest; he is always sublime."

66 J. H., "Milton and His Epic," *Sharpe's London Magazine,* n.s. VI, 309. Also see "Shades of the Dead," *Athenaeum,* No. 90 (15 July 1829), pp. 441–42, in which the author says that the national admiration of Milton can only be found in "the dignity of his character."

67 Carlyle, *The Life of Schiller, Works,* XXV, 44. The Milton quotation is from his "An Apology for Smectymnuus."

68 "Milton and the Commonwealth," *British Quarterly Review,* X, 254.

69 "The Youth of Milton," *Edinburgh Review,* CXI (April, 1860), 315–17.

70 Tulloch, *English Puritanism and Its Leaders,* p. 244.

71 Dowden, "Milton: Civil Liberty," in *Puritan and Anglican,* pp. 20–21.

72 Edmonds, *John Milton,* p. iv.

73 [Masson], review of *The Works of John Milton, North British Review,* XVI, 297.

74 Keightley, *John Milton,* p. 156.

75 Tulloch, *English Puritanism and Its Leaders,* p. 167.

76 Dowden, "Milton: Civil Liberty," in *Puritan and Anglican,* p. 175.

77 Blunt, "Milton," in *Essays Contributed to the Quarterly Review,* p. 48.

78 William Gifford, *The Plays of Philip Massinger* (London, 1813), pp. lxxx–lxxxi.

79 Charles Kingsley, *Plays and Puritans* (London and New York, 1890), p. 10.

80 *Ibid.,* pp. 68–69.

81 Garnett, *Milton,* p. 12.

82 Frederick Denison Maurice, *The Friendship of Books and Other Lectures* (London and New York, 1886), p. 257.

83 Dowden, "Milton: Civil Liberty," in *Puritan and Anglican,* p. 184.

84 Tulloch, *English Puritanism and Its Leaders,* pp. 270–71.

85 Richardson, *Explanatory Notes and Remarks on Milton's Paradise Lost,* p. 229.

86 Raleigh, *Milton,* p. 145.

87 Mrs. Jameson, *Memoirs of the Loves of the Poets,* pp. 250–51.

88 Garnett, *Milton,* p. 196.

89 John Robert Seeley, "Milton's Poetry," in *Lectures and Essays* (London, 1870), p. 154. Originally appeared in *Macmillan's Magazine,* XIX (March, 1869), 421.

90 George Gilfillan, "The Genius of Milton," *Tait's Edinburgh Magazine,* XV (1848), 511–22.

91 Edmond Scherer, "Milton," in *Essays on English Literature,* trans. from the French by George Saintsbury (New York, 1891), p. 121.

92 Eneas Sweetland Dallas, *The Gay Science* (London, 1866), II, 150–52. H. A. Taine in his *History of English Literature,* unlike Dallas, agrees with Masson that Milton was governed by idea, principle, rigid obedience to an ideal. "Two special powers lead mankind," he wrote, "impulse and idea: the one influencing sensitive, unfettered, *poetical souls,* capable of transformations, like Shakespeare; the other governing active, combative, heroic souls, capable of immutability, like Milton. The first are sympathetic and effusive; the second are concentrative and reserved" (pp. 503–504). (Italics added.)

93 Dallas, *The Gay Science,* II, 204.

94 *Ibid.,* p. 203.

95 Maurice, *The Friendship of Books,* p. 246.

96 Pattison, *Milton,* pp. 14–15. See also Tulloch, *English Puritanism and Its Leaders,* pp. 169–70; Bowles, *Life of Ken,* I, 79–80.

97 Pattison, *Milton,* p. 30.

98 Arnold, "A French Critic," in *Mixed Essays,* p. 259.

99 W. J. Courthope, *A History of English Poetry* (6 vols., New York and London, 1895–1910), III, 412.

100 Arthur Windsor, "Milton:—His politics, Prose Writings, and Biographers," in *Ethica* (London, 1860), p. 52.

101 Brydges, *Life of Milton,* p. xxxvii.

102 Bayne, "John Milton," *Contemporary Review,* XXII, 438.

103 Raleigh, *Milton,* p. 45.

104 Edward Dowden, "The Idealism of Milton," *Contemporary Review,* XIX (1872), 201.

105 Masson, *The Life of John Milton,* VI, 840. Also see J. R. Green, *A Short History of the English People* (New York, 1886), chap. 8, "Puritan England," especially pp. 459–60, 582–83.

VI. MILTON AND TENNYSON

1 Hallam Tennyson, *Alfred Lord Tennyson, a Memoir by His Son* (2 vols., London, 1897), I, 36. This passage, from Edward Fitz-Gerald's notes, also recalls that Tennyson considered Milton's similes, "one about the 'gunpowder ore,' and the other about 'the

fleet,' as the grandest of all similes."

2 *Memoir*, II, 284. Tennyson considered the poetic diction of Milton to be "even finer than that of Virgil, 'the lord of language.' "

3 Milton, "Ad Patrem."

4 Milton, "The Reason of Church Government," in *Prose Selections*, ed. Merritt Y. Hughes (New York, 1947), p. 107.

5 *Ibid.*

6 Tennyson, "Merlin and the Gleam," in *Works*, p. 550. Lascelles Abercrombie says in "Tennyson," in *Revaluations* (London, 1931), p. 66, that this poem "is the confession of one whose life was indistinguishable from his art." Earlier (p. 61), he notes that "like Virgil's, Tennyson's life was wholly given to his art. He had no other life."

7 Milton, "An Apology for Smectymnuus," in *Prose*, p. 154.

8 Milton, "Church Government," in *Prose*, p. 106.

9 Milton, "Elegy VI," in *Minor Poems*, p. 171.

10 *Ibid.*

11 "Church Government," in *Prose*, p. 104.

12 *Memoir*, I, 12.

13 Frederic Harrison, "Tennyson," in *Tennyson, Ruskin, Mill* (London, 1900), p. 4.

14 *Ibid.*, p. 9.

15 *Memoir*, I, 16.

16 Charles Tennyson, *Alfred Tennyson* (New York, 1949), p. 32.

17 Charles Tennyson, "Tennyson Papers, I. Alfred's Father," *Cornhill Magazine*, CLIII (March, 1936), 292.

18 *Memoir*, I, 7–9.

19 *Memoir*, I, 9.

20 See *Memoir*, I, 7–20 *passim*.

21 Charles Tennyson, *Tennyson*, p. 40.

22 Alfred Tennyson, *Unpublished Early Poems*, ed. Charles Tennyson (London, 1931), p. vi.

23 Charles Tennyson, *Tennyson*, p. 49.

24 Charles Tennyson, "Tennyson's Unpublished Poems," *Nineteenth Century*, CIX (1931), 370.

25 *Ibid.*

26 Full text of "Armageddon" is found in Charles Tennyson's edition of Tennyson's *Unpublished Early Poems*, pp. 6–15.

27 Thomas Lounsbury, *The Life and Times of Tennyson* (New York, 1915), p. 59.

28 Tennyson, *Works*, p. 761.

29 *Ibid.*, p. 765.

30 *Ibid.,* p. 767.
31 *Memoir,* I, 36.
32 Hallam, *The Writings of Arthur Hallam,* ed. T. H. Vail Motter (New York, 1943), p. 304.
33 *Memoir,* I, 46.
34 Hallam, *Writings,* p. 193.
35 *Memoir,* I, 91.
36 Hallam, *Writings,* p. 235.
37 T. Wemyss Reid, *The Life, Letters, and Friendships of Monckton Milnes* (2 vols., London, 1890), I, 72.
38 *Memoir,* I. 139–40.
39 J. F. A. Pyre, *The Formation of Tennyson's Style* (Madison, 1921), p. 20.
40 *Ibid.,* p. 236. See Appendix A, "Tennyson's Early Diction," pp. 225–43, where Pyre lists pages of parallelisms and reminiscences of Milton.
41 This poem was first published by Charles Tennyson in 1931 in "Unpublished Poems, I," *Nineteenth Century,* CIX, 380.
42 Tennyson, *Works,* pp. 778–80.
43 Both Professor Pyre and Edward P. Morton treat in some detail the blank verse of this poem. See especially Morton's *The Technique of English Non-Dramatic Blank Verse* (Chicago, 1910), p. 21. Morton says (pp. 124–25) that *Timbuctoo* is "the nearest to *Paradise Lost* in its proportion of run-on and endstopt lines."
44 Charles Tennyson, "Unpublished Poems, I," *Nineteenth Century,* CIX, 370–71.
45 See W. D. Paden, *Tennyson in Egypt* (Lawrence, Kansas, 1942), p. 146, for a detailed treatment of these two passages.
46 Text is in Tennyson, *Works,* pp. 787–88.
47 *Memoir,* II, 518.
48 *Memoir,* II, 503.
49 J. W. Mackail, *The Springs of Helicon* (London, 1909), p. 160.
50 G. Robert Stange, "Tennyson's Garden of Art," *PMLA,* LXVII (1952), 733.
51 *Ibid.,* p. 734.
52 *Ibid.,* pp. 734–35.
53 Charles Tennyson, *Tennyson,* p. 451.
54 *Memoir,* I, 152.
55 *Memoir,* II, 421.
56 Saintsbury, in *A History of English Prosody* (3 vols., London, 1908), III, 270–71, said, "We shall have to wait for Tennyson before we can find any thirdsman for Shakespeare and Milton in

the use of this device; but it was Milton who distinctly indicated it as a special resource to English poets."

57 *Ibid.*, p. 184.
58 *Ibid.*, p. 201.
59 William M. Rossetti, *Dante Gabriel Rossetti*, I, 191.
60 *Memoir*, I, 184.
61 *Memoir*, II, 96–97.
62 Charles Tennyson, *Tennyson*, p. 329.
63 *Memoir*, II, 518 ff., contains these comments and many others re *Paradise Lost.*
64 *Memoir*, II, 414.
65 Epilogue, "To the Queen," ll. 65–66.
66 *Lycidas* ll. 64–66.
67 *In Memorian*, section LXXIII, l. 11; section LXXVII, ll. 1–4. Sections LXXII–LXXVII are on the subject of fame.
68 Section LXXIII, l. 12; section LXXV, ll. 12–20.
69 Patmore, "In Memoriam," *North British Review*, XIII (1 August 1850), 534.
70 John Addington Symonds, *Letters and Papers* (New York, 1923), p. 20.
71 *Memoir*, II, 69–70.

VII. MILTON THE ARTIST—THE LATE VICTORIAN VIEW

1 Francis Thompson, "John Milton," *The Academy*, LI (27 March 1897), 358.
2 Eliot, of course, has more recently dropped the charge that Milton "is an unwholesome influence," and has said that Milton is a great poet "whom poets today might study with profit" ("Milton II" [1947], *On Poetry and Poets*, p. 169). I am merely indicating here what seems to me to be a kind of cycle in Milton criticism which came full circle with the rejection in our time of Milton's artistry.
3 John Keats, *The Complete Poetical Works* (Boston, 1899), p. 39.
4 Raleigh, *Milton*, p. 123.
5 Walter Pater, "Robert Elsmere," *Essays from "The Guardian,"* in in *The Works of Walter Pater* (London, 1901), p. 67. The review appeared 28 March 1888.
6 Noel Annan, *Leslie Stephen* (Cambridge, Mass., 1952), pp. 162, 165.

7   Pattison, *Milton,* p. 201.
8   Raleigh, *Milton,* p. 83.
9   Bagehot, "Milton," in *Literary Studies,* I, 194.
10 Pattison, *Milton,* p. 200.
11 Bagehot, "Wordsworth, Tennyson and Browning," in *Literary Studies,* II, 321–23.
12 Pattison, *Milton,* p. 188.
13 John Ruskin, *Sesame and Lilies,* Lecture III, *Works,* XVIII, 157.
14 Garnett, *Milton,* p. 158.
15 Matthew Arnold, "A French Critic," in *Mixed Essays* (London, 1907), p. 261.
16 Augustine Birrell, "John Milton," in *Obiter Dicta, Second Series,* pp. 45–46. Also compare Garnett, p. 153: "It is easy to represent 'Paradise Lost' as obsolete by pointing out that its demonology and angelology have for us become mere mythology. This criticism is more formidable in appearance than in reality. The vital question for the poet is his own belief, not the belief of his readers. If the Iliad has survived not merely the decay of faith in the Olympian divinities, but the criticism which has pulverized Achilles as a historical personage, 'Paradise Lost' need not be much affected by general disbelief in the personality of Satan, and universal disbelief in that of Gabriel, Raphael, and Uriel."
17 For instance, Raphael's speech to Adam, V, 564:

> ... for how shall I relate
> To human sense th' invisible exploits
> Of warring Spirits; how without remorse
> The ruin of so many glorious once
> And perfet while they stood; how last unfold
> The secrets of another world, perhaps
> Not lawful to reveal? Yet for thy good
> This is dispens't, and what surmounts the reach
> Of human sense, I shall delineate so,
> By lik'ning spiritual to corporal forms,
> As may express them best, though what if Earth
> Be but the shadow of Heav'n, and things therein
> Each to other like, more than on earth is thought?

Milton believed that God revealed himself and his ways to man in the Scriptures, not necessarily as he actually is, but as he, aware of our human, finite capacities, wishes us to conceive of him. In chapter two, "Of God," in the *De Doctrina,* he made this perfectly clear when he wrote that "to know God as he really is, far transcends the powers of man's thoughts. . . . God therefore has made as full a revelation of himself [in the Bible] as our minds can conceive, or the weakness of our nature can bear." Therefore, Milton concluded, "Our safest way is to form in our minds such a conception of God, as shall correspond with his own delineation and representation of himself in the sacred writings. For granting that both in the literal and figurative descriptions of God, he is exhibited not as he really is, but in such a manner as may be within the scope of our comprehensions, yet we ought to entertain such a conception of him, as he, in condescending to accommodate himself to our capacities, has shewn that he desires we should conceive."

18 "English Poets and Oxford Critics," *Quarterly Review,* CLIII. (1882), 450.

19 Keightley, *John Milton,* p. 451.

20 H. Rawlings, "The Transfigured Theology of 'Paradise Lost,' " *Westminster Review,* CLIII (January, 1900), 32.

21 *Ibid.,* 32.

22 *Ibid.,* 33.

23 *Ibid.*

24 *Ibid.,* 35.

25 *Ibid.*

26 *Ibid.,* 41.

27 *Ibid.*

28 The late Victorian rejection of Milton's thought and the emphasis on his art was anticipated, however, by Walter Savage Landor, Leigh Hunt, Walter Bagehot, and Matthew Arnold. For example, Landor, in the Imaginary Conversation between Southey and Landor, said: "Averse as I am to everything relating to theology, and especially to the view of it thrown open by this poem [*Paradise Lost*], I recur to it incessantly as the noblest specimen in the world of eloquence, harmony and genius."—"Southey and Landor," in *Works,* V, 280.

Similarly, Bagehot, who thought that the theology of *Paradise Lost* was vitiated by the fact that it was founded upon a political transaction, was of the opinion that no book was really greater if style and artistry were the basis for decision: "Perhaps no style ever written by man expressed so adequately the conceptions of a mind so strong and so peculiar; a manly strength, a haunting atmosphere of enhancing suggestions, a firm continuous music, are only some of its excellencies."—"Milton," in *Literary Studies*, I, 194.

Although Matthew Arnold grew peevish and irritable when he thought of Milton's Puritan theology, he had nothing but praise for Milton's artistry: "Shakespeare himself, divine as are his gifts, has not, of the marks of the master, this one: perfect sureness of hand in his style."—"A French Critic," in *Mixed Essays*, pp. 266–67.

29   Dowden, *Puritan and Anglican*, pp. 182–83.

30   See *Three Friends: Memoirs of Digby Mackworth Dolben, Richard Watson Dixon, Henry Bradley* (London, 1932), p. 139.

31   Notice, for instance, the word choice in one section of Raleigh's biography: There *Paradise Lost* stands, he cried, "like some enchanted palace, a monument to the miraculous skill of its maker—just stands and no more: but that it should stand at all is the marvel, seeing that it is spanned on frail arches over the abyss of the impossible, the unnatural, and the grotesque."—*Milton*, pp. 122–23.

32   Raleigh, *Milton*, p. 88.

33   Recall Morris' statement which I quoted earlier to the effect that in Milton's works he found combined the two things which he hated most: "cold classicism and puritanism."

34   Gardner, *Gerard Manley Hopkins* (2 vols., London, 1948), II, 211.

35   Landor, "Southey and Landor," in *Works*, V, 286.

36   Landor, "Abbé Delille and Landor," in *Works*, VII, 214.

37   See William Bradley, *The Early Poems of Walter Savage Landor* (London, n.d.), for a study of Milton's influence on Landor's early poetry.

38   See Arnold's letter to J. D. Coleridge in Ernest Hartley Coleridge's *Life and Correspondence of J. D. Coleridge* (2 vols., London, 1904), I, 210–11.

39   Lionel Trilling, *Matthew Arnold* (New York, 1949), p. 144n.

40   Arnold, "Milton," in *Essays in Criticism, Second Series* (London, 1898), p. 66. Cf. Arnold's statement in an early letter to Clough: "Those who cannot read G[ree]k sh[ou]ld read nothing but Milton and parts of Wordsworth; the state should see to it."—*The Letters of Matthew Arnold and Arthur Hugh Clough*, ed. H. F. Lowry (London and New York, 1932), p. 97.

41   L. Binyon, "Robert Bridges and the Poetic Art," *Bookman*, LIV (1918), 144.

42 See Raymond Williams' discussion of this new meaning which the word "artist" acquired in *Culture and Society* (London, 1958), p. xv.

43 [Coventry Patmore], "English Metrical Critics," *North British Review,* XXVII (August, 1857), 160.

44 I quote from Reuben Brower's introduction to *Alexander Pope* (Oxford, 1959), pp. 1–2.

45 Frederick Pollock, "John Milton," *Fortnightly Review,* LIV (1890), 519.

46 Albert J. Guerard says this in *Robert Bridges* (Cambridge, Mass., 1924), p. 259.

47 J. W. Mackail, *The Springs of Helicon,* (London, 1909), p. 200.

48 John Addington Symonds, "The Blank Verse of Milton," *Fortnightly Review,* XXII (n.s., XVI),(1874), 781.

49 Hopkins, *Further Letters of Gerard Manley Hopkins,* ed. Claude Colleer Abbott (London, 1956), p. 144.

50 Bridges, *Milton's Prosody* (London, 1921), p. 51.

51 Symonds, "Blank Verse," *Fortnightly Review* XXII (n.s., XVI), 767–68.

52 *Ibid.,* 768, 769, 771.

53 Patmore, "Metrical Critics," *North British Review,* XXVII, 131–32.

54 *Ibid.,* 161.

55 T. S. Eliot, "Milton, II" (1947), in *On Poetry and Poets,* p. 183.

56 Gardner, *Gerard Manley Hopkins,* II, 113.

57 Quoted in Frederick Page, *Patmore, A Study in Poetry* (London, 1933), p. 147.

58 Quotations from *Chatworth* are found in Basil Champneys, *Memoirs and Correspondence of Coventry Patmore* (2 vols., London, 1900), I, 46–47.

59 See J. C. Reid, *The Mind and Art of Coventry Patmore* (London, 1957). On page 58 he says that Patmore's poetry earlier was much more Wordsworthian, "the later more Spenserian, Biblical and Miltonic." Also see p. 272.

60 *The Correspondence of Gerard Manley Hopkins to Richard Watson Dixon,* ed. Claude Colleer Abbott (London, 1955), p. 13.

61 *Ibid.,* p. 17.

62 Bridges, *Collected Essays* (30 vols., London, 1927–36), XII, 22. The original review appeared in the *Times Literary Supplement,* 1 April 1909.

63 Guerard, *Robert Bridges,* p. 45.

64 See *Three Friends,* p. 17.
65 Bridges, *Essays,* XII, 22.
66 In *Poetical Works of Robert Bridges* (6 vols., London, 1898), I, 54–55.
67 *Ibid.,* p. 5. For a specific, detailed discussion of Milton's influence on Bridges, see Guerard, *Robert Bridges,* pp. 45–47; also see Chaps. 6, 9, and Appendix A.

✑ Bibliography

This bibliography does not include all the works mentioned in the notes. It contains (1) the nineteenth-century commentaries on Milton which the author found most useful; (2) some Miltonic religious epics referred to in the text which through the years have been largely forgotten; and (3) a group of fictional works discussed in the text in which Milton appears as a character. Recent Milton criticism has been omitted, since it can readily be found in bibliographies such as David H. Stevens' *Reference Guide to Milton*, Harris F. Fletcher's *Contributions to a Milton Bibliography*, and Calvin Huckabay's *John Milton: A Bibliographical Supplement, 1929–1957*.

NINETEENTH-CENTURY COMMENTARIES

Aikin, J[ohn]. "An Essay on the Poetry of Milton," in *The Poetical Works of John Milton from the Text of Doctor Newton: with a Critical Essay by J. Aiken, M.D.* 3 vols. Philadelphia: Benjamin Johnson, 1804.

Arnold, Matthew. *Essays in Criticism, Second Series.* London: Macmillan, 1898.

———. *The Letters of Matthew Arnold and Arthur Hugh Clough.* Edited with an introductory story by Howard Foster Lowry. London and New York: Oxford University Press, 1932.

———. *Mixed Essays.* London: Smith, Elder, 1903.

"A Talk about Sonnets." *Blackwood's Edinburgh Magazine*, CXXVIII (August 1880), 159–74.

Bagehot, Walter. *Literary Studies.* 2 vols. Everyman's Library edition. London: J. M. Dent, n.d.

Bayne, Peter. *The Chief Actors in the Puritan Revolution.* London: James Clarke, 1879.

———. "Milton." *Contemporary Review,* XXII (1873), 427–60.

Birrell, Augustine. *Obiter Dicta, Second Series.* New York: Scribners, 1894.

Blunt, Rev. J. J. *Essays Contributed to the Quarterly Review.* London: John Murray, 1860.

Bridges, Robert. *Collected Essays, Papers, etc.* 30 vols. London: Oxford University Press, 1927–1936.

———. *Milton's Prosody.* London: Oxford University Press, 1921.

———. *Three Friends: Memoirs of Digby Mackworth Dolben, Richard Watson Dixon, Henry Bradley.* London: Humphrey Milford, 1932.

Brooke, Stopford A. *Milton.* Classical Writers series. London: Macmillan, 1879.

Browning, Elizabeth Barrett. *The Book of the Poets.* Vol. VI of *The Complete Works of Elizabeth Barrett Browning.* 6 vols. New York: Crowell, 1901.

———. *The Letters of Robert Browning and Elizabeth Barrett Browning, 1845–1846.* 2 vols. New York: Harper and Bros., 1899.

Byrdges, Egerton. "Life of Milton," in *The Poetical Work of John Milton.* Boston: Phillips, Sampson, and Co., 1855. Reprinted often in various nineteenth-century editions of Milton's works.

Busby, Stanhope. *Lectures on English Poetry to the Time of Milton.* London: Whittaker, 1837.

Carlyle, Thomas, *Two Notebooks of Thomas Carlyle, from 23rd March 1822, to 16th May, 1832.* Edited by Charles Eliot Norton. New York: The Grolier Club, 1898.

Carpenter, William. *The Life and Times of John Milton.* London: Wakelin, 1836.

The Chartist Circular. Edited by William Thomson. Glasgow: W. and W. Miller. All the issues which I examined—from 28 September 1839 to 9 July 1842—were found bound together in Special Collections, Columbia University Library.

Coleridge, Samuel Taylor. *Coleridge's Shakespearean Criticism.* Edited by Thomas M. Raysor. 2 vols. Cambridge: Harvard University Press, 1930.

Cooper, Thomas. *The Life of Thomas Cooper Written by Himself.* London: Hodder and Stoughton, 1872.

Cox, F. A., the Rev. "Milton's *Paradise Lost* Considered with Reference to its Theological Sentiments and Moral Influence." *Journal of Sacred Literature,* I (April 1848), 236–57.

Dallas Eneas S. *The Gay Science.* 2 vols. London: Chapman and Hall, 1866.

Darwin, Charles. *Autobiography.* Edited by Nora Barlow. New York: Harcourt, Brace, 1959.

De Vere, Aubrey. *Essays Chiefly On Poetry.* 2 vols. London: Macmillan, 1887.

De Vere, Sir Aubrey. *Sonnets* [with a *Memoir* by his son]. London: Basil Montagu Pickering, 1875.

Dowden, Edward. "The Idealism of Milton." *Contemporary Review,* XIX (1872), 198–209.

———. *Puritan and Anglican: Studies in Literature.* London: Kegan Paul, Trench, 1900.

———. *Transcripts and Studies.* London: Kegan Paul, Trench, 1888.

Downing, John, editor. *Testimonies and Criticisms Relating to the Life and Works of John Milton.* St. Austell: W. B. Luke, 1903.

Edmonds, Cyrus R. *John Milton: A Biography Especially Designed to Exhibit the Ecclesiastical Principles of That Illustrious Man.* London: A. Cockshaw, 1851.

"English Poets and Oxford Critics." *Quarterly Review,* CLIII (1882), 431–63.

"Ernest, the Chartist Epic." *Quarterly Review,* LXV (1840), 190–91.

Fletcher, Robert. "An Introductory Review," in *The Prose Works of John Milton.* London: Westley and Davis, 1835.

Froude, James Anthony. *Short Studies of Great Subjects.* 5 vols. New York: Scribner's, 1908.

Froude, Richard Hurrell. *Remains.* 2 vols. London: J. G. and F. Rivington, 1838.

Garnett, Richard. *Life of John Milton.* London: Walter Scott, 1890.

Gilfillan, George. "The Genius of John Milton." *Tait's Edinburgh Magazine,* XV (August 1848), 511–22.

———. *A Gallery of Literary Portraits.* Edinburgh: James Hogg, 1845.

———. *A Second Gallery of Literary Portraits.* Edinburgh: James Hogg, 1850.

———. *A Third Gallery of Portraits.* Edinburgh: James Hogg, 1854.

Gillies, Mrs. Leman. "Milton and His Daughters." *People's Journal,* V (1848), 227–28.

Glassford, James. *Lyrical Compositions Selected from the Italian Poets.* Edinburgh: A. and C. Black, 1846.

Hales, John W. "Milton's Macbeth." *Nineteenth Century,* XXX (December 1891), 919–32.

Hallam, Arthur. *The Writings of Arthur Hallam.* Edited by T. H. Vail Motter. New York: Modern Language Association, 1943.

Hallam, Henry. *Introduction to the Literature of Europe.* 4 vols. New York: Sheldon, 1863.

Harrison, Frederic. *Among My Books: Centenaries, Reviews, Memoirs.* London: Macmillan, 1912.

———. *The New Calendar of Great Men.* London: Macmillan, 1892.

———. *Tennyson, Ruskin, Mill and Other Literary Estimates.* London: Macmillan, 1900.

Hayley, William. *The Life of Milton.* Dublin: William Porter, 1797. An influential biography during the nineteenth century.

Hood, Edwin Paxton. *John Milton: the Patriot and Poet, Illustrations of the Model Man.* London: Partridge and Oakey, 1852.

Hopkins, Gerard Manley. *The Correspondence of Gerard Manley Hopkins and Richard Watson Dixon.* Edited by Claude Colleer Abbott. London: Oxford University Press, 1955.

———. *Further Letters of Gerard Manley Hopkins.* Edited by Claude Colleer Abbott. London: Oxford University Press, 1956.

———. *The Letters of Gerard Manley Hopkins to Robert Bridges.* Edited by Claude Colleer Abbott. Second Revised Edition. London: Oxford University Press, 1955.

———. *The Note-books and Papers of Gerard Manley Hopkins.* Edited by Humphry House. London and New York: Oxford University Press, 1937.

Ivimey, Joseph. *John Milton: His Life and Times, Religious and Political Opinions.* New York: D. Appleton, 1833.

J. H. "Milton and His Epic." *Sharpe's London Magazine,* n.s. VI (1855), 308–11.

Jameson, Mrs. Anna Brownell (Murphy). *Memoirs of the Loves of the Poets.* Boston and New York: Houghton Mifflin, 1888. First published under the title: *Loves of the Poets.* London, 1829.

[Jeffrey, Francis]. Review of Wordworth's *Poems. Edinburgh Review,* XI (October 1807), 214–31.

Keble, John. *Keble's Lectures on Poetry, 1832–1841.* 2 vols. Translated from the Latin by Edward K. Francis. Oxford: Clarendon Press, 1912.

Keightley, Thomas. *An Account of the Life, Opinions, and Writings of John Milton with an Introduction to Paradise Lost.* London: Chapman and Hall, 1855.

Kingsley, Charles. *Literary and General Lectures and Essays.* London and New York: Macmillan, 1898.

———. *Plays and Puritans and Other Historical Essays.* London and New York: Macmillan, 1890.

"The Life and Poetry of Milton." *Eclectic Magazine,* XXX (November 1853), 364–72. Review originally appeared in *Hogg's Instructor.*

Macaulay, Thomas B. "A Conversation between Mr. Abraham Cowley and Mr. John Milton," in Vol. VII of *The Works of Thomas Macaulay.* 8 vols. London: Longmans, Green, 1879.

———. *Critical and Historical Essays.* Everyman's Library edition. 2 vols. New York: E. P. Dutton, 1907.

Masson, David. *Essays Biographical and Critical: Chiefly on English Poets.* Cambridge: Macmillan, 1856.

———. *The Life of John Milton: Narrated in Connexion with the Political Ecclesiastical, and Literary History of His Time.* 6 vols. New York: Peter Smith, 1946.

———. Review of *The Works of John Milton. North British Review,* XVI (February 1852), 295–335.

Maurice, Frederick Denison. *The Friendship of Books and Other Lecturers.* London and New York: Macmillan, 1886.

McDouall's Chartist and Republican Journal, Nos. 1–27 (April 2–October 2, 1841). In the Seligman Collection, Columbia University Library.

McNicoll, Thomas. "Sacred Poetry: Milton and Pollok," in *Essays on English Literature.* London: B. M. Pickering, 1861.

Milner, George. "A Note on Two Sonnets by Milton and Tennyson." *Manchester Quarterly,* XI (1892), 356–59.

Milton, John. *Milton's Sonnets.* Edited by A. W. Verity. Cambridge: Cambridge University Press, 1916.

———. *The Sonnets of John Milton.* Edited by Mark Pattison. New York: D. Appleton, 1896.

"Milton and the Commonwealth." *British Quarterly Review,* X (August 1, 1849), 224–54.

"Milton and Shakespeare." *Scots Magazine,* LXXXV (1820), 241–48.

"Milton's Rib-bone." *Notes and Queries,* First Series, V (April 17, 1852), 369.

Montgomery, James. "Memoir of John Milton with Strictures on his Genius and Writings," in *The Poetical Works of John Milton.* New York: Leavitt and Allen, n.d.

Newton, the Rev. Thomas. "Life of Milton," in *The Poetical Works of John Milton.* 4 vols. Oxford: Parker, 1824. An influential biography during the nineteenth century.

Noble, James Ashcroft. "The Sonnet in England." *Contemporary Review,* XXXVIII (September 1880), 446–71.

[Patmore, Coventry]. "English Metrical Critics." *North British Review,* XXVII (August 1857), 127–61.

———. "In Memoriam." *North British Review,* XIII (August 1850), 532–55.

Pattison, Mark. "John Milton," in *The English Poets.* II. Edited by Thomas H. Ward. 5 vols. New York: Macmillan, 1908.

———. *Milton.* English Men of Letters Series. London: Macmillan, 1879.

Pollock, Frederick. "John Milton." *Fortnightly Review,* LIV (1890), 510–19.

Raleigh, Walter. *John Milton.* London: Edward Arnold, 1900.

Rawlings, H. "The Transfigured Theology of 'Paradise Lost.'" *Westminister Review,* CLIII (January 1900), 32–41.

Roberts, Samuel. *Milton Unmasked.* London: Longman, Orme, Brown, Green and Longman, 1844.

Rossetti, William Michael. *Dante Gabriel Rossetti, His Family-Letters with a Memoir.* 2 vols. Boston: Roberts Bros., 1895.

St. John, J. A. "Preface" to *The Prose Works of John Milton.* Edited by J. A. St. John. 5 vols. Bohn Library Edition. London, 1848.

Scherer, Edmond. *Essays on English Literature.* Translated from the French by George Saintsbury. New York: Scribner's, 1891.

Seeley, John Robert. *Lectures and Essays.* London: Macmillan, 1870.

———. "Milton's Poetry." *Macmillan's Magazine,* XIX (March 1869), 407–21.

"Shades of the Dead." *Athenaeum,* No. 90 (July 15, 1829), pp. 441–42.

Shairp, J. C. "Keble's Estimate of Milton." *Macmillan's Magazine,* XXXI (1875), 554–60.

Stebbing, the Rev. H[enry]. "Memoir of Milton's Life and Writings" in *The Complete Works of John Milton.* New York: D. Appleton, 1845.

Symonds, John Addington. "The Blank Verse of Milton." *Fortnightly Review,* XXII [n.s. XVI] (December 1, 1874), 767–81.

———. *Letters and Papers.* New York: Scribner's, 1923.

Tennyson, Hallam. *Alfred Lord Tennyson, a Memoir by his Son.* 2 vols. London: Macmillan, 1897.

Thompson, Francis. "John Milton." *Academy,* LI (March 27, 1897), 357–58.

Tomlinson, Charles. *The Sonnet, Its Origin, Structure, and Place in Poetry.* London: John Murray, 1874.

Tulloch, John. *English Puritanism and Its Leaders*. Edinburgh and London: Blackwood and Sons, 1861.

Wallace, Robert. *Antitrinitarian Biography: or Sketches of the Lives and Writings of Distinguished Antitrinitarians*. 3 vols. London: E. T. Whitfield, 1850.

"William Herbert's Imitation of Milton." *Monthly Review*, CXLV (1838), 392–93.

Willmott, Robert Aris. *Lives of the Sacred Poets, Second Series*. London: John W. Parker, 1838.

Wilson, John. *Noctes Ambrosianae*. [Edited by J. F. Ferrier]. 4 vols. Edinburgh and London: W. Blackwood and Sons, 1855–1856. The *Noctes* comprises the first four volumes of *The Complete Works*.

Windsor, Arthur. *Ethica: or, Characteristics of Men, Manners, and Books*. London: Smith, Elder, 1860.

"The Youth of Milton." *Edinburgh Review*, CXI (April 1860), 312–47.

MILTONIC EPICS

Atherstone, Edwin. *The Fall of Nineveh, a Poem*. [First six books]. London: Baldwin and Cradeck, 1828.

Bailey, Philip James. *The Mystic and Other Poems*. Boston: Ticknor and Fields, 1856.

[Heraud, John Abraham]. *The Descent into Hell*. London: John Murray, 1830.

———. *The Judgement of the Flood*. London: James Fraser, 1834.

Herbert, William. "Attila, or the Triumph of Christianity, a Poem in Twelve Books," Part One in *Attila, King of the Huns*. London: Bohn, 1838.

Montgomery, Robert. *The Messiah. A Poem in Six Books*. London: John Turrill, 1832.

———. *The Omnipresence of the Deity*. Eleventh edition. London: Maunder, 1830. First edition appeared in 1828.

———. *Satan, a Poem*. London: Maunder, 1830.

———. *A Universal Prayer; Death; A Vision of Heaven; and A Vision of Hell, etc.* Second edition. London: Maunder, 1829.

Pollok, Robert. *The Course of Time, a Poem in Ten Books*. 2 vols. Edinburgh and London: Wm. Blackwood and T. Cadell, 1827.

Ragg, Thomas. *The Deity. A Poem*. In Twelve Books. With an introductory essay by Isaac Taylor. Second edition. London: Longman, Rees, Orme, Brown, Green, and Longman, 1834.

FICTIONAL WORKS

Manning, Anne. *Mary Powell* and *Deborah's Diary*. Everyman's Library edition. New York: Dutton, n.d.

Myers, Ernest. *The Puritans*. [a drama]. London: Macmillan, 1869.

Ring, Max. *John Milton and His Times*. Translated from the German by F. Jordan. New York: D. Appleton, 1868. Originally published as *John Milton und seine Zeit. Historischer Roman*. Frankfort on the Main, 1857.

Shorthouse, Joseph Henry. *John Inglesant*. London: Macmillan, 1910. First edition appeared in May, 1881.

[Smith, Horatio]. *Brambletye House; or, Cavaliers and Roundheads*. 3 vols. Boston: Wells and Lilly, 1826.

Vetch, Major. *Milton at Rome; a Dramatic Piece*. Edinburgh: James Hogg, 1851.